BECOMING A STRONG AND IMMOVABLE WIFE

How God Helped Me Face the Hard Seasons of Marriage with Confidence

VERONIC TURGEON

WESTBOW
PRESS®
A DIVISION OF THOMAS NELSON
& ZONDERVAN

This book is a work of non-fiction. Unless otherwise noted, the author and the publisher make no explicit guarantees as to the accuracy of the information contained in this book and in some cases, names of people and places have been altered to protect their privacy.

WestBow Press books may be ordered through booksellers or by contacting:

WestBow Press
A Division of Thomas Nelson & Zondervan
1663 Liberty Drive
Bloomington, IN 47403
www.westbowpress.com
844-714-3454

Because of the dynamic nature of the Internet, any web addresses or links contained in this book may have changed since publication and may no longer be valid. The views expressed in this work are solely those of the author and do not necessarily reflect the views of the publisher, and the publisher hereby disclaims any responsibility for them.

Any people depicted in stock imagery provided by Getty Images are models, and such images are being used for illustrative purposes only.
Certain stock imagery © Getty Images.

Scripture quotations are taken from the Holy Bible, New International Version®. NIV®. Copyright © 1973, 1978, 1984 by International Bible Society. Used by permission of Zondervan. All rights reserved.

Scriptures marked as NLT are taken from the Holy Bible, New Living Translation, copyright © 1996, 2004, 2015 by Tyndale House Foundation. Used by permission of Tyndale House Publishers Inc., Carol Stream, Illinois 60188. All rights reserved.

Scripture taken from The Holy Bible, The ESV® Bible (The Holy Bible, English Standard Version®). ESV® Permanent Text Edition® (2016). Copyright © 2001 by Crossway, a publishing ministry of Good News Publishers. The ESV® text has been reproduced in cooperation with and by permission of Good News Publishers. Unauthorized reproduction of this publication is prohibited. All rights reserved.

ISBN: 978-1-6642-9100-3 (sc)
ISBN: 978-1-6642-9101-0 (hc)
ISBN: 978-1-6642-9099-0 (e)

Library of Congress Control Number: 2023901602

Print information available on the last page.

WestBow Press rev. date: 02/24/2023

"I know the Lord is always with me.
I will not be shaken,
for He is right beside me."

Psalm 16:8

I lovingly dedicate this book to my late Mom.
She endured many hard seasons
in life and her marriage.
Her prayer was that you would
be encouraged that God is enough
to go through the hard seasons of life,
small or big.

CONTENTS

A WORD FROM PHIL

Dear Reader,

My wife shares through this book many of our ups and downs through the first twenty years of our life together. She shares very personal and intimate details about how I treated her and the sins I committed which greatly affected our marriage and her.

Know that she has my full consent to write every word you will read. I hope and pray you will realize how powerful and almighty our God is and how He is able to transform a life.

"And I am convinced that nothing can ever separate us from God's love.
Neither death nor life, neither angels nor demons, neither our
fears for today nor our worries about tomorrow—not even
the powers of hell can separate us from God's love.
No power in the sky above or in the earth below—indeed,
nothing in all creation will ever be able to separate us from the
love of God that is revealed in Christ Jesus our Lord."

Romans 8:38-39 (NLT)

I invite you to read this book which I hope will inspire you to follow God wholeheartedly, either for the first time or to renew your commitment to Him.

I am blessed that my wife still stands by my side! Be assured He can transform you as He has transformed both of us.

May the Lord bless you,
Phil Turgeon

THE LIGHTHOUSE: A REFUGE FROM THE STORM

When I look at the cover picture, I see so many biblical concepts represented. First and foremost, it is a shelter from the storm. It doesn't take you out of the storm, but provides shelter through the storm.

"God is our refuge and strength,
always ready to help in times of trouble.
So we will not fear when earthquakes come and
the mountains crumble into the sea.
Let the oceans roar and foam.
Let the mountains tremble as the waters surge!"

(Psalm 46: 1-3, NLT)

"Those who live in the shelter of the Most High
will find rest in the shadow of the Almighty.
This I declare about the Lord:
He alone is my refuge, my place of safety;
He is my God, and I trust Him."

(Psalm 91: 1-2, NLT)

"The Lord is my rock, my fortress, and my savior;
my God is my rock, in whom I find protection.
He is my shield, the power that saves me,
and my place of safety."

(Psalm 18:2, NLT)

The lighthouse itself can take quite the beating through the fiercest storms, but because of its solid foundation, it remains standing.

"Be on guard. Stand firm in the faith. Be courageous. Be strong."

(1 Corinthians 16:13, NLT)

The lighthouse provides much needed light and a sense of direction through storms and darkness.

"You are the light of the world—like a city on
a hilltop that cannot be hidden.
No one lights a lamp and then puts it under a basket. Instead,
a lamp is placed on a stand, where it gives light to everyone in
the house. In the same way, let your good deeds shine out for all
to see, so that everyone will praise your heavenly Father."

(Matthew 5:14-16, NLT)

Jesus never promised to take us out of the storms of life, but He did promise He would never leave us or forsake us (Hebrews 13:5) and that He is **always** with us (Matthew 28:20). Do not let the storms in your life destroy you, rather draw nearer to God in these troubled times and surrender to the winds of adversity and pain so that you might be refined and radiant with joy. (Psalm 34:5)

ACKNOWLEDGEMENTS

To my dear Lord and Savior Jesus Christ who is the reason for this book. He is worth every breath, every tear, every joy, and every second of your life. Nothing will satisfy you but Him. I cannot wait to see Him face to face! My one and only desire is that, through this book, you get to know Him more intimately and are freed from whatever is holding you back from experiencing the fullness of what God has in store for your life.

To my husband, my best friend. How far we have traveled in 22 years! Even through all our ups and downs, I would not trade you for anyone else. May we always follow the One who saved us. Love you more.

To my children: Maxime, Sophie, Elyse, Alexandre, Xavier, Amelie and Sebastien. Thank you for willingly offering to take on some of my chores, watching over the little ones, and cooking delicious meals that I could complete this project. I love you so much words cannot fully express it.

To my mother who passed away during the final stages of the publication. She encouraged me to continue the mission God had entrusted me. One month before her passing, she shared how she wished that thousands of women would be encouraged to keep trusting God through the hard seasons of their lives and their marriages. Her prayer was that God would use this book to bring many to Himself.

To Louise, my dear godly friend, who was the first to encourage me to put my story into words. Thank you for being there every time I needed it. I have understood who Jesus is through many of your actions in my early years as a believer.

To Ron Rudd, who was the first to trust us with sharing our testimony. You have been a blessing and an encouragement in our walk and through the writing of this book. May God reward all your hard work at keeping marriages and families strong.

To Ann Rudd, who worked many hours at editing this book. Thank you for your precious help and your prayers. May God reward your beautiful servant and godly heart.

To Stephen Priddle, who greatly helped with the editing and enthusiastically encouraged us to pursue this project. Thank you for believing in us! May God reward your labor in strengthening marriages and families.

To Lise Guertin, who is our family's prayer warrior. Thank you for all the prayers you have poured into this project and the great love you have for our family. May God bless you as you are an incredible encouragement.

To Steve and Robyn Strongitharm, John and Louise Hammer, Henry and Heather Berghuis, and Lise Guertin. Thank you for being the first readers, and giving us your precious feedback.

To the Kingdom Brothers, my husband's men's group, who have faithfully prayed for our family and this project. Thank you! Your prayers have been answered in powerful ways.

To Westbow Press, who made the publication of this book possible. Thank you to a most kind and encouraging staff! I have learned much through your guidance.

To Tony and Mylene Joyal, who faithfully obeyed God many years ago and bought me my first Bible. It was indeed a lamp to my feet and a light on my path. Much love to you and your beautiful family.

To Sylvain and Chantalle Renaud and their three boys (now grown men), who showed us great love and patience in the years before our coming to Christ. Thank you!

To all my Sisters in Christ who prayed this book would transform the lives of many: Andrée-Anne Kemp, Marise Cassivi, Marcia Olynyk, Yvette Malebranche, Jacynthe Guertin, Elisabeth Labelle, Yen Priddle, Vinita Baker and the many more who secretly took their prayers to the Throne of Grace on behalf of this project. Thank you!

INTRODUCTION: STRONG AND IMMOVABLE

"Because he loves me," says the Lord, "I will rescue him,
I will protect him, for he acknowledges my name.
He will call on me, and I will answer him;
I will be with him in trouble,
I will deliver him and honor him.
With long life I will satisfy him
and show him my salvation."

Psalm 91:14-16 (NIV)

Strong and immovable ... two powerful words. And thanks be to God, they have become my words and my story. And I pray with all of my heart they can be yours too. Whether you know the Lord personally or are exploring the Christian faith, this world can be hard. Some periods of our lives can seem harder than others. So how do we navigate through them? How do we do life when all seems lost or broken? Where do we find strength to function, even have joy, in the midst of trials and difficulties?

Those were some of the questions I asked myself and looked for in the hardest seasons of my life. It took me some time to find them, but I did. In the beginning, I have to be honest, I was looking for a quick fix. Something like, "God, how fast can You get me out of this?" But with time, I learned you cannot rush through these seasons of life or rush God. God allows them for a purpose. A much greater purpose. And if you will trust Him, He can reveal Himself to you in ways you never imagined. That's what happened to me. I got to a point where I cried out to Him and willingly gave Him all of myself. All of it. The good, the bad, and the ugly. And that's when an amazing, intimate, closer relationship began... the greatest relationship I had ever had or will ever have - one with our great God, the Creator of the universe, an intimate relationship with my Father in Heaven.

For the past four years, I have been praying for this book. God has laid it on my heart to share my story with you, so you can know how much He loves you. How much He desires to connect with you, to help you. If you would turn all of yourself over to Him. His strength can be yours. His love can be yours. His joy can be yours. His salvation is yours to receive.

"Trust in the Lord with all your heart and lean
not on your own understanding;
in all your ways acknowledge Him,
and He will make your paths straight."

Proverbs 3:5-6 (NIV)

Will you trust Him? I have found it is the only right and safe way to navigate through life. Let me share with you how I found this strength.

"So if you are suffering in a manner that pleases God,
keep on doing what is right, and trust your lives to the God who created you,
for he will never fail you."

1 Peter 4:19 (NLT)

CHAPTER ONE

MY STORY

The reason I share my background story at the forefront of this book is that I want you to understand where I came from. Before I even begin sharing with you what God has laid on my heart and taught me, I want to be transparent and honest with you. I am far from being perfect. I am a sinner just like any other human being on the face of the earth. Personally, I find it is much easier to relate to someone when I can catch a glimpse of who they are.

> *"Not that we are competent in ourselves*
> *to claim anything for ourselves,*
> *but our competence comes from God."*
>
> *2 Corinthians 3:5 (NIV)*

I was born in 1980 in Silver Springs, Maryland. My father worked for External Affairs (later re-named Foreign Affairs & International Trade) of Canada and was stationed there at the time. Due to complications, my mother ended up having a C-section at my birth. As she was cuddling me in her arms three days after the delivery, the doctor came into her room and gently asked her what she was saying to me. She went on to say how much she loved me and how I was hers. To her surprise, the doctor then proceeded to tell her that I was only lent to her for a period of time, but that I really belonged to God. At the time, she didn't think anything in particular about his remarks and went on with life. But this comment stuck with her.

As I grew up I heard her tell me this story a number of times. My parents did not believe in any particular religion and therefore, never taught or forced any religious beliefs on us . They always told us we could

1

choose what to believe. So I carried this story with me for 27 years before it started to make any sense.

During those 27 years, I lived far away from God. He wasn't important to me and I cared more about living for myself than listening or obeying God. Even though I had some foundation of morals in my life, it was full of sin like everyone else. Lying, stealing, sexual immorality, strife, jealousy and more. All of those sins were a part of my life to some degree. I would have times of happiness, but deep down inside I felt empty. It continually took more pleasures, more hobbies, more things to try to fill that emptiness.

My childhood was spent traveling around the world as we followed my father's postings in different embassies. After we left Silver Springs, we lived in Thailand for two years before we came back to Canada so my father could get further training for his work. We spent three years in Canada before we were posted to Beijing, China in 1986. I was six years old at the time and our family had grown. I had two other siblings. My sister was three years younger than me and my brother was 5 years younger. I have great memories of China. We visited many landmarks and learned much of the country's history. I even got to walk on the Great Wall of China seven times! What a privilege! Working for External Affairs enabled my parents to hold and attend many receptions. My father already had alcohol issues, and it seemed that during those years, his drinking increased. He was present, but was never a strong figure of leadership. He left those responsibilities to my mother. She was strong and competent, but I could sense even then, that things were not right. My parents worked very hard so we never lacked anything and our basic needs were always met. But our family relationships and connections were not strong. Little did I know, things were not going to get better.

We lived in Beijing for three years until June 1989. The weeks leading up to the tragic events of June 4th, 1989, are etched in my mind forever. We lived only four blocks away from Tiananmen Square, in downtown Beijing. On June 4th, we were evacuated from China by the government of Canada. Being 9 years of age at the time, I can vividly remember each detail of those days coming back to Ottawa. Even to this day, I could still give you a detailed account of those moments. My mother courageously took care of us as we made it back to Canada safe and sound. At the end of that summer, we moved to Dakar, Senegal in Africa for the next four years.

Our family grew even more distant from each other during those years. My mother was on many committees and organized many activities for the children of the embassy of which we would be included. But the growing relational distance between my father and her affected us all. My father's alcohol issues grew substantially during our years in Africa. At times he would sneak out of the house without telling my mother where he was going. He started swearing at us when he was drunk. And my mother started slowly slipping into depression. She was a strong woman, but even at a young age, I could sense it was taking a toll on her.

The happiest times in Africa were when extended family would visit from Canada. My friends became my way of escape. And it was during those years that I began having sleepovers. The activities I was involved in because of these relationships were some of the worst experiences of my life. Being around 11, I started having some questions about sexuality and my friends were who I turned to for answers. And also at this time I discovered my father's pornographic magazines. My parents found out about it, but laughed it off and excused it as life experiences. But this had a huge impact on me. Seeing those very graphic pictures of naked women, changed the way I thought about myself. Was this how I was supposed to look and act? An evil seed was planted in my mind and heart, the impact of which I would not fully realize for another 20 years.

In 1993, our family moved from Africa back to Canada. My father decided to change his field of service to computers, as the internet had launched a few years before and there were many new opportunities in this field in the Department of Foreign Affairs. I was now 13. Having moved so often, I never had friends for more than 2 to 4 years. Starting in a new high school was frightening for me. Having always been in international private schools before, it was the first time I would set foot in a public school. It was weeks before anyone spoke to me.

By then, my dad was drinking every day. My mother struggled to make ends meet. We were often short on money and I ended up needing to wear some of my great aunt's clothes. As you can imagine, they were not the trendy clothes others were wearing. So I became somewhat of a laughing stock in my class. Acne changed my looks, which made me shy away from being with people. I always loved learning, books and school, so I was often teased for being the teacher's favorite. I eventually made friends with a few people, but they were not a good influence on me.

Being miserable at home, because my parents were arguing so often, I would try to find belonging and acceptance from my peers. I began smoking and "drinking" beer. I disliked the taste of alcohol and did not want to end up like my father, so I would pretend to drink and when the opportunity would present itself, I would throw it down the drain. But I kept smoking until 2005. During this time I was also introduced to the occult through a Ouija board. Most of the people at my school were "playing" it, so I decided to try it out too. We all thought it was innocent fun and it did seem like that for a while. But it was everything short of innocent fun. The more we played, the more spooked I became by the game and the strange things that were happening. So after three years of playing it off and on, I stopped and got rid of it. If I had known how dangerous it was, which I do now as a Christian, I would never have played with it!

Those years between the ages of 13 and 15 were tainted with immense pressure to be sexually active with boys my age. Even though I had a few boyfriends, I resisted the urge to give in to these pressures. These relationships never lasted more than about two or three weeks. And having a boyfriend did not fill the loneliness I felt. I felt more and more miserable on the inside. I wanted something better in life but did not know where to look for it. When I experienced my first breakup at 13, I was not ready for the intensity of emotion that came with it. In hindsight, I know I was too young to be involved in a romantic relationship. But my parents did not mind and at the time I thought it was all part of life as so many others my age would do the same.

In 1995, we moved again which meant another change of schools in grade 10. New school meant new friends and a new start. I did make friends, but soon fell into the same pattern of peer pressure controlling my life. In contrast to my social life, I loved school very much and my studies kept me going. I was a good student and had good grades. I started dreaming of having a bright and successful future. One that, of course, included a handsome husband and a family of my own. I had been babysitting since age 13 and loved kids.

In 1997, after graduating from high school, I went to college to study psychology and history. I loved reading *Discover* magazine during those years. Two years into college, I made a presentation on the evolution of man and how scientists had then discovered a possible new species in Spain which was causing them to reconsider the chronology of their view of our evolution as a species. For some reason, this made me think about what I had been taught since childhood. A seed of doubt about evolution was planted in my mind. However, I didn't have a strong desire or make any effort to research my doubts at that time.

During my college years, my parents separated. When we got back to Canada in 1993, my father started traveling on his own to different embassies throughout the world for his new position. He began carrying on adulterous affairs on numerous occasions. My mother pleaded with him to get counseling for their marriage, but he refused and after a long five years of mediation, they were divorced. I have many regrets from the following three years. Having no close relationship with my mother, her being increasingly depressed over her life circumstances and our family being torn apart, I tried to escape the pain in many ways. I became sexually active and quite obsessed with trying to please men. I started going to bars. My earlier aversion to alcohol was gone and even though I was never drunk, I still consumed enough to be in good spirits every time. I continued this lifestyle for the next three years and then tired of the life I had made for myself. It only temporarily filled an emptiness in my aching heart and distracted me from my pain.

In 2001, at 21 years of age, the doctor found out I had cancerous cells in my uterus and I was informed it would be near impossible for me to have children. But I miraculously recovered over the next few weeks, but was told it would be hard to conceive. It devasted me back then, because I truly loved children and really wanted to be a mother one day. That same year, I met Phil in a pool hall. My friends and I loved playing pool. Phil was handsome and looked every bit like the man of my dreams. After a few days, he asked me out and, of course, I said yes. In that same year, we both got really tired of the bar and pool hall life and quit going. Soon after this, I moved into my first apartment and life seemed to be looking up over the next six months. I was in love and life was good! At that time, I worked in two different shoe stores where two of my co-workers were

Christians. They would share their faith with me occasionally and I would ask questions about their beliefs.

As my relationship with Phil continued, I noticed he owned a massive pornographic magazine collection. This made me feel insecure, but since most men around me liked porn, I convinced myself it was normal. Even though I was already sexually active, it didn't seem right to me. So I pleaded with him to get rid of them. Since he already had an eight year old daughter, from a previous relationship, who was sleeping in the same room as him, I urged him to do it for her. He refused.

We moved in together in 2003 and that's when I noticed he was drinking beer every day. He would not look drunk at all, but since my father was an alcoholic, I was concerned that he would end up like my father. We started fighting. We ended up yelling at each other every time a disagreement came between us. Until one day. We were yelling back and forth and after 20 minutes, Phil stopped and looked at me. He asked me if I remembered why we were fighting. I couldn't remember. We started to laugh! It taught us a lesson and we vowed to never yell at each other again. If we felt inclined to do so, we would take a step back and calm down. It was, in fact, the last time we yelled at each other.

In the meantime, because I was disturbed by having them in my home, I decided to throw away all his pornographic magazines and movies while he was at work. But before I did, I decided to watch two of the movies to try to understand why he liked pornography so much. I thought that maybe if I knew what this was all about, I could help him see the wrong in it. How wrong I was! It made me feel worse. A lot worse! It also taught me a valuable lesson that I still hold to this day. It is often best not to know all the little details. When he came home, I told him what I had done and to my surprise he wasn't mad, and I thought to myself, "Maybe there was a God after all", like my coworkers had said. I learned many years later that he had gone back into the dumpster to collect some of them back and hide them elsewhere. Oh, what foolishness grows out of our unconfessed sins!

Two years later, in 2005, I became pregnant with our first child. At that time, Phil's family did not take the news with joy. Phil had been vocal with his family about not wanting any more children after he had a daughter when he was 19 and she was now 11. His family accused me of having forced Phil to have another child. Those were hard times. I remember meals where his family would be there, we would all be sitting at the same table, but no one would speak to me except Phil. I was sad, but not discouraged. I had hoped that things would get better. What helped me get through this difficult time was that Phil was very supportive and took my side. However, his drinking seemed to get worse. It made me very anxious. I felt like I was living my parents' situation all over again. Around that time, one of my coworkers and friend, Mylene, bought me my first Bible and I started reading it for myself. Even though I did not believe yet, Psalm 91 became one of my favorite Bible passages. When I would read it before bedtime it would calm me greatly.

During the pregnancy not only was I stressed with our family situation and Phil's alcoholism, but his previously occasional hobby of playing computer games, during the pregnancy became an everyday event. I "coped" with this added stress by gaining a whopping 70 pounds during those nine months. With Phil's pornography and lust issues, and my pain and anxiety, our intimacy became non-existent. I began to sink into depression, longing for a closer relationship and connection with my husband. The only help I had was one of my former Christian coworkers who at the time was there for me.

Maxime was born in February of 2006. My heart was so thankful! Having to care for a little one of my own brought back some of my happiness and lifted my spirits. But he would not sleep for any long period of time! He was chronically constipated and cried a lot. When he was three weeks old, he developed a virus which included a high fever for a week. The doctors had no answers for us. We had to wait for the fever to go down and hope that he would not suffer brain damage. When it subsided we went home and it took three to four more months for him to sleep more than three or four hours a night. Phil's older daughter, Roxanne, who was living with us at the time, became very insecure. She thought we were replacing her in the family. We tried to reassure her this wasn't the case, but having Phil and Roxanne's mother on very bad terms already, made our family situation very tense. She ended up leaving us to go live with her mother full time. Phil was heart-broken.

As you can imagine, I was exhausted, and I had no patience with Phil. A huge chasm was growing between us. I had a hard time trying to understand his side. After over six months of not having any sexual relationships, I decided to confront him. He admitted that my weight gain turned him off completely and he did not feel as attracted to me as before. I was devastated and cried and cried. But deep down inside there was some relief and I was at least thankful he was honest with me. This motivated me to join a gym and work at increasing my activity. It greatly helped my depressive state. After a few weeks, I was beginning to feel "normal" emotionally. It helped Phil and me to start to reconnect. As our intimacy improved, to my surprise, Phil decided to quit playing computer games. He had realized he did not want to make some of the same mistakes he had made with his daughter Roxanne. He had not been very present for her and had not done many father-daughter activities. Thankfully, Phil never went back to computer gaming.

That's when I learned I was expecting again. Maxime had just turned 8 months. I was thrilled when I learned we were expecting a girl! We moved shortly after to a three bedroom townhouse. My family took the news with great joy, but again, Phil's parents did not. I started to wonder if I would ever really get along with them.

During that second pregnancy, Phil's drinking got worse. He could literally drink 24 beers and still walk straight and not feel drunk. His body would absorb the alcohol so well. It was worrying me quite a bit. Sophie was born in July of 2007. What a joy she was to care for and a great sleeper. I recovered much faster this time around.

Personally, during this time, I had one big problem though...nagging. I had always dreaded becoming a nagger like my mother and that's exactly what happened. One morning I confronted Phil as to why he was leaving an hour earlier for work in the past month. He told me that my nagging was so annoying to him that he was leaving an hour earlier just to get some peace. That hurt! But that is exactly what I needed to hear. I had become my mother. I commited from that day on to stop nagging and start watching my words more closely.

Things improved between us for a few months. But then I found out that our savings account was missing a couple thousand dollars. Phil had just begun his own renovation business a few months earlier and that account was for paying our income taxes. When I confronted Phil about this he admitted that he had started drinking during his work hours and that for lunch he would regularly play slot machines. This was a discouraging blow for me. We had two young children, our eldest was 21 months and our daughter was 4 months old. One night, as I was nursing Sophie I poured out my heart to God. I told Him the drinking needed to stop. I didn't want to raise our children in this mess. When I was done nursing, I felt a peace like I had never felt before wash over me. It felt like God was close to me. The realization that He was real and was there with me was so clear that I made a decision that same night, to give my life completely to Him. I asked him to forgive my sins and put my trust in Him as my Savior and Lord. I knew from the Bible reading I had done and what my coworkers had shared with me that I could talk to God anywhere and anytime. I knew that I needed a Savior because I could not save myself by my own efforts. The feeling of peace that swept over me that night confirmed everything I had been told about God to be true.

I then felt that I could approach Phil with an ultimatum. A couple of days later I told him he needed to take a couple days away from us to think things through and decide what he really wanted. It was either the kids and me without the alcohol, or the alcohol and no family. I didn't want a separation and I definitely did not want a divorce! After going through that with my parents, I knew all too well the damage it causes. But I also knew I couldn't continue life the way we were going. I also told him we could no longer have sexual relationships until we made things right with God. Knowing it could drive him down the road back to pornography or infidelity, I prayed for him almost daily. Even with all our struggles Phil assured me he loved me very much. And so on November 11, 2007, Phil stopped drinking. And he never went back. The temptation left him. Even though Phil was not living for God at the time, in hindsight, we knew it had to be Him who helped Phil stop in such a way. It was such a complete change I never had any suspicion that he drank after that day. It was truly a miracle!

I started going to an English church in the summer of 2008. And I was so grateful for how supportive Phil was. He encouraged me to keep going, even though he did not want to go himself. He noticed that I was changing. And the more I changed, the more he became curious about God. So much so that a year later, in the summer of 2009, he surrendered his life to God. And he proposed! We approached a pastor at our church and were married soon after, as we realized we shouldn't be living together unmarried, let alone have sexual relationships before marriage.

Now I knew our troubles were all over. We were both Christians and married and that meant we were now right with God. Things were going to be wonderful! But four days after our wedding I found out Phil was still viewing pornography. To say the least, I was not happy. My thoughts that all my problems were solved and everything would be perfect were shattered. After much discussion, he told me he would stop and I believed him. But without my knowledge he continued his habit. It was a very powerful addiction for him.

In December of 2009, Phil had an operation on his back for two herniated discs. While he was recuperating I took care of him every day. The first weeks, he could not even wash himself. I had to do everything for him. God gave me the strength and grace to care for him. That same month, I had to take my mother to the emergency room for an infection in her foot, aggravated by her diabetes and her neglect to take her medicine. The doctors said she was on the verge of losing her foot. Miraculously, she recovered, but she too needed care and came to live with us while she recuperated.

To make things more complicated at the time, I also was running a daycare, as Phil was convinced that both parents absolutely need to work. I was caring for four other children in addition to my two. The days were busy and very demanding. I was giving four people baths every night! But, with the Lord's help I was able to stay joyful and not lose hope that He was with me. Having been "alone" most of my childhood, I did what I knew best - I persevered.

When my father had left my mother, she was forced to work all the hours she could get. So at a young age I had to grow up very quickly and learn how to take care of a household. Those experiences were very helpful later in life as God used it to prepare me for being a homemaker.

In January 2010, about a month after my husband and my mother's operations, I was finally getting some relief as their mobility was improving. My mother moved back to her apartment and I felt life was getting back into a routine. Until I got a phone call from the hospital. I was told my paternal grandmother was dying. I was devastated! I was so close to her. I would confide in her sometimes. For the past five years, I would visit her every week with the children, helping her in any way I could. I felt like I was losing the only person in my family I ever felt close to. That morning I was told to come quickly. I had talked to her the night before, and she had told me how much she loved me and that she felt the end was near. Sadly, I didn't make it to the hospital on time that morning to say a final goodbye.

Phil was an enormous support during those times and this brought us a bit closer. I got back into my routine and we decided I should close the daycare that summer. I wanted to devote my time to raising our children and spending more quality time with them. I had been through a lot of trials and my family was a priority for me, so I needed to make the necessary arrangements to reflect those values.

The next year, in 2011, we decided to get baptized together to make a public confession of our decisions to follow Jesus. And around that same time we were surprised to learn I was expecting again. I never thought I would have any other children, but God had other plans for us. Phil then started thinking God would fix all our marriage problems, but as a young Christian, he did not realize that God expected him to put in some effort into making those changes. I knew this wasn't true but God needed to show this to Phil.

Elyse was born in October of 2011. She was such an amazing baby, slept through the night almost right out of the hospital. I loved being a mother of three, and being able to care for my own children.

During the following year, in 2012, I had some nagging thoughts that my faith was not as serious as it should be. Some painful things happened in the relationship with one of my former Christian coworkers which affected our friendship. This left me feeling empty and that I was not growing spiritually. I recognized that I was feeling a heavy burden of guilt. I would read the Bible, attend an occasional women's study and still found no help for these feelings.

Neither Phil nor I had any godly mature people in our lives. Our lives just felt like a wheel turning and turning without any real changes, and I was so tired of it all!

One day, while reading my Bible, I came across John 8:31-32: "If you hold to my teaching, you are really my disciples. Then you will know the truth and the truth shall set you free." I thought, "I do not feel free, God!" It occurred to me then that I was not as serious about my faith as

I should be. I confessed this to God and again became very aware of His Holy Presence that day.

Another day during that time, God spoke to me again. I was complaining bitterly to Him about our marriage and all the things that were not going well. Actually, I was complaining about all the wrong things Phil was doing. That's when I clearly heard His voice in my mind, "Really? You can't find one good thing to say about this man?" I responded, "No, because we are in this mess because of him!" Suddenly, God brought to my mind Romans 3:23: " For **ALL** have sinned and fall short of the glory of God." He challenged me to write a list of all the good things Phil was doing and to start thanking him for those things. So my list began:

> He always gets the mail.
> He always takes care of the trash and the recycling.
> He helps with the dishes and the house chores.
> He is a really hard worker and we do not lack anything.

> And so it continued.

What that did to me that afternoon was to help me realize that I was not seeing my husband the way God sees him. I was focusing more on the negative things and couldn't see the positives God was changing in Phil. After this revelation my attitude toward my husband started changing greatly. As I thanked Phil for simple things like taking the trash out and helping with the dishes, I also started seeing him in a different way, and my heart softened toward him.

The following months, as I drew closer to God, I started praying for my husband, for our marriage and for our family regularly.

On a Sunday morning in January of 2013, as I was expecting our fourth child and feeling very tired, Phil took our three other children to church and I stayed home. I decided to listen to a sermon series at home during that time. It was titled "Living in the Will of God" by Charles Price of People's Church, Toronto. I started listening to the second sermon in the series, which was titled "His ways are not our ways".

After fifteen minutes, God got a complete grip on my heart. I got on my knees and wept. I then surrendered all of my life, the messes I had made of it, and particularly my marriage to Him. I felt so free! It was like a burden was lifted off my shoulders. I wasn't the one in control of everything anymore - He was.

In the following weeks I began to see that my husband was not the enemy after all. And that Phil's sins, that he was captive to, were tools that Satan was using to destroy our marriage. The devil was the enemy, not Phil. My prayers centered on asking God to release the enemy's grip on Phil and to draw him closer to Himself. It took another three and a half years before I saw the answer to those prayers, but I did not lose hope. I loved God so much and I saw Him changing my heart so I knew He could change Phil also.

This didn't mean that every day was a blissful experience. Some days were hard, but I clung to the hope that God gave me and I drew closer to Him during those times. I grabbed His Hand and decided to never let it go. God impressed on me that one day I would have to face Him and give an account of what I did in His name, including my marriage (Romans 14:12). That gave me great motivation to represent Him as best as I could, starting in my own marriage.

The other thing that began to happen is that the closer I moved toward God, the more our lives changed. I also began to set clear boundaries for my life and say 'no' to certain demands so I would have more time for the important things in this season of my life. God was teaching me discernment and that I did not need to help or rescue the people around me every time there was a need. A lot of the situations these people were facing were because of their own doing, and my actions were enabling them to stay irresponsible. This decision created a lot of tension in my life and relationships that year. Certain relationships became more challenging that year and some people treated me unkindly. I had become too serious for them and they would make fun of the fact that we had started homeschooling. My decision to focus on my husband and children and stop constantly feeling responsible to rescue others had an impact on my family as well. This caused some distance between us for a couple of years. My sister, however, remained supportive of us through this time. Phil's family, unlike before, embraced the changes and it gave me opportunities to talk with my mother-in-law more about God.

But God did not leave me without friends and support in other ways.

He sent an older Christian lady, Louise, who greatly encouraged me in my faith and my marriage. We would pray together regularly and I grew closer to God because of her friendship and help. I came to realize that when God becomes your central focus, when you truly seek Him with all you have, then He will carry you through anything. And in the midst of pain and hardship I could have joy.

One night, in the fall of that year (2013), Phil and I were both watching a movie after the kids had gone to bed and I had been feeling low that day. I was nursing Alex, our fourth born and I was praying. Even though I was sitting next to Phil I felt miles away from him. To this day, I do not remember what movie we were watching. But I clearly heard God's voice in my mind again, "It will become worse before it will be better." How kind was God to prepare me for this by revealing part of His plan.

That year Phil's lust of the eyes issue became so bad, I felt I could almost hear his thoughts when he would look at a woman. But along with the pain, there was great peace and hope in my heart. During this time, I struggled with insecurities about my physical image. This was another area that God would work on with me over the next few years - the ability to see myself as He sees me.

God had taken me through so much, I refused to quit now. So I drew closer to Him through His Word and through intense prayer. I was shocked to discover in the summer of 2014 that Phil had never stopped looking at pornography. He had quit for over a year, but was pulled back into the addiction. This time, because of my stronger relationship with God, I was not devastated. It forced me to hold the hand of my Heavenly Father even tighter. So I increased my prayers and asked Louise to join me in this. She was such a blessing! Never once did she or her husband, John, ever judge or condemn us. They would accept Phil and me just as we were.

That's when I decided to do something bold. Phil had broken his wedding ring at work and had gotten it repaired, but it wasn't the same anymore. It was bent and looked funny. So I secretly saved up some money to buy him a new one. A couple months later, I gave it to him. He was very surprised and asked me why I had decided to do such a thing, knowing he was still hurting me. I told him that I love him, and had resolved to stay with him no matter what, and I would keep praying for him to be released from his pornography and lust addictions.

As God had warned me, things did not get better. Phil got a smartphone. Over the next two years, I felt God protected me from knowing all the details surrounding Phil's addictions. I felt Him tugging at my heart to come closer to Him. I started reading the Bible several times a day and memorized many verses. I kept my focus on God and on what He had called me to do as a wife and mother. I had four young children to take care of and I was resolved to do it to the best of my abilities, drawing on His strength. I was also serving in our church's Awana children's program. I poured myself into everything God had allowed in my life to serve Him with all of my heart.

Reading became a source of inspiration and growth for me during this time. Biographies about Christian heroes and martyrs became a blessing for me in my spiritual walk. Compared to some of the trials these people had gone through would put my marital issues in perspective making them seem insignificant. Their boldness and courage inspired me. Helen Berhane, Adoniram and Ann Judson, Samuel Morris, Dietrich Bonhoeffer, Perpetua and many more are some of my favorites. Richard Wurmbrand's story was also an encouragement to me. Being in a communist prison for 14 years, cruelly mistreated and never once did he retaliate against his accusers. He loved them like Jesus. In light of this example, who was I to complain about my marriage? It got me thinking about trials and difficulties in life and I began to see them in a different light. The shortness of life became a vivid reality for me and I didn't want to miss out on God's best in the years that He was giving me. In addition to biographies I found strength and encouragement from other mature and godly authors as well.

So I pressed on and worked diligently with all He had so graciously given me. A husband, four children, the chance to homeschool them and show them the path to our Savior made me a blessed woman!

In February of 2016, after two consecutive miscarriages, the Lord brought about another blessing in our lives when our little Xavier was born.

When Xavier was around seven and a half months old, I discovered that Phil had been lying to me about many things. The smartphone had indeed made pornography worse since he could access it anywhere and anytime. After I discovered this, Phil came to the point where he realized he was destroying himself, his marriage, and his relationship with God. As hard as it was, and it was very hard, Phil confessed his sins to me, even admitting he cheated on me three times. One of them I knew about from before we had children, but the two other times I did not know. It was incredibly hard to hear this, but it was freeing at the same time. Like the brick wall that was between us had finally fallen! The enemy had lost. Phil came clean and repented from his sins before God and me. My prayers that I had been crying out before God for three and a half years had been answered in a powerful way. I was grateful that God gave me the strength to be diligent and persistent to bring my requests to him, even when I didn't see much change in Phil.

Phil suddenly started changing in a very dramatic way. It was astounding! He took dramatic steps to gain my trust. He smashed his smartphone and went back to a flip phone with no internet connection. He confessed his sins to a close friend and to other trustworthy men. He went to talk with a professional for one session to see if there were other things he could do. He asked me to change our laptop password and not to give it to him. And the times he needed to use it, he would use it in the same room I was in and only when I was present. And we have continued these practices even to this day.

Over the next months, he started taking his role as a follower of Christ more seriously and spent more time in God's Word every day. He got on his knees in front of all our children and asked forgiveness for all that he did and asked God if He could help restore our marriage. He prayed for me and for our children. I did what I could to support him in this. I made him a verse pack to help him get through his days at work and strengthen himself spiritually as he fought this battle to stay pure. Phil went from being obsessed with other women to loving me in ways I did not think were possible for him.

The changes in me were slow at first since Phil had broken my trust so many times. With time God showed me I could trust my husband again. My husband is my best friend now. I wouldn't dream of spending life with anybody else. God more than restored our marriage for which I am so grateful!

What God had shown me through these years was that on our wedding day, we had made vows to each other: "For better **OR** for worse, for richer **OR** for poorer, in sickness **OR** in health, **till death do us part.**" These vows we had indeed spoken in His presence (Psalm 50:14b). I wanted to honor those vows, but not for my sake or Phil's sake, but to bring glory to our God. As Dietrich Bonhoeffer once said: "Actions must follow what one believes, else no one could claim to believe it." How could I have claimed all these years that I was a Christian and not follow through with those beliefs even when life was hard?

In 2018, we welcomed our sixth child, Amelie, and for the first time Phil was there for me throughout the pregnancy and afterward. He even took three weeks off of work after her birth in order to help me recuperate, something he had not done before. With our other five children, I was on my own three days after their birth. It was a great time for our family. The children loved having him around. He began to be the father that they needed.

With the incredible things God did for us since the fall of 2016, everything felt like a new beginning. Our marriage, our family, our home and our ever growing relationship as two becoming one and our relationships with God are all new.

At that point I thought all my marital struggles had been exposed. Little did I know the most hurtful sins my husband committed were about to be discovered.

In the summer of 2019, I learned that we were expecting another child. I had just finished nursing our sixth born, Amelie, and felt quite exhausted from our house building and move a year and a half ago. For the first time, I struggled with feelings of not wanting to be pregnant anymore. I was not thinking in terms of abortion, but like the fact that I was getting too old and thought we already had enough children to care for. It was strange as I always rejoiced in the precious children God chose to send our way. I had never before questioned His leading about the size of our family. I always rejoiced in learning we were expecting another child. After many weeks of praying, I realized my feelings were a spiritual attack and began to wonder what blessing lay ahead for our family. I knew too well Satan often tries to discourage us before God brings about a blessing in our lives.

Mid-pregnancy, in January of 2020, we learned that Sebastien was going to be born with Down Syndrome and a severe heart defect. There were very high chances of him not surviving the four required months before surgery. The hole in his heart was very large. When my obstetrician announced the news to Phil and me, we felt an incredible peace wash over us and knew deep in our hearts God was in total control of this whole situation. We never doubted from that day.

May 2020 came and our little sunshine was born and within less than 2 minutes was rushed to ICU for poor breathing and poor cardiac rhythm. There began for us a five and a half weeks journey traveling daily to the intensive care unit to see and hold our precious little boy. We saw God's hands in many ways through this entire time. In June he was finally able to come home and meet his siblings. What a great family reunion that was! The following months were filled with almost no sleep, pumping breastmilk for Sebastien as he could not be nursed because of the strain it put on his heart. I made trips to the hospital and to his pediatrician weekly to ensure his health would be optimal for his open heart surgery planned for early September. And by God's grace, He enabled us to help Sebastien reach all the requirements for that surgery. What a miracle!

Before the surgery took place, I slept every night in Sebastien's room as he needed constant supervision due to his breathing and cardiac issues. I had never felt so attacked by Satan as during those months. Somehow I knew this wasn't only due to Sebastien and writing this book. I spent countless hours at night on my knees and seeking direction from the Lord in those difficult months. Early August, one month before Sebastien's planned surgery, the Lord impressed on my heart to fervently pray for my husband as he needed to confess other hurtful sins.

Then just at the end of August, as I was feeding Sebastien before his bedtime, and watching a sermon from Dr. Stanley titled *"The Dark Moments in Our Life."* which emphasized that the dark moments will last only as long as it takes for God to accomplish His purposes.

The next morning we got ready to have lunch and a visit with one of Phil's aunts, who is a sweet, mature, godly woman. We had been anticipating this day for a while. She is always such an encouragement to be around and one of the few other people in both our families who is walking with the Lord.

When we got there, she gave me a long ago crocheted picture in a frame which she felt that the Lord was impressing on her heart to give to me. The frame had the following verse inscribed on it: *"The angel of the Lord encamps around those who fear him, and he delivers them."* (Psalm 34:7, NIV). I was so delighted to be able to visit someone during the

Covid-19 pandemic and for the restrictions to permit us to do so that I did not make sense of what the Lord was doing at the moment. But as we headed back home I strongly sensed the Holy Spirit preparing me for an important conversation that night. So we put the children to bed early and I retreated to pray for a few minutes before facing Phil, asking the Lord to watch over the words of my mouth and the motives of my heart. I felt so calm and could feel the awesome presence of God in our home in a very powerful way.

Through that conversation Phil ended up confessing that he had not only committed adultery three times but many more as he struggled with an addiction to prostitutes. Early in his life he was introduced to a nude camping site. He was immersed in sexual immorality at an age where no child should be exposed to such sins. It led him to pornography at the age of 10 and woke an appetite for sexuality at a tender age where his innocence should of been protected. I felt such compassion and hurt for him that night. Still my heart aches to know how much brokenness he suffered because of the situations he was involded in during his childhood and Satan's exploitation of those. This prostitute addiction followed him even after our wedding and his early desire to follow Christ. He admitted to having been unfaithful over 70 times in the span of our first 18 years together. When he was done confessing, we heard the sound of a mighty rushing wind around our home. The Spirit of God then passed through our home and in between Phil and I. It was incredible! God's presence so powerfully filled our home, it was palpable! We were weeping so much because of the love we felt overflowing our hearts that night. Heaven is going to be an amazing place as the Lord enabled us to experience a tiny piece of what it is to stand in His magnificence. Phil has been experiencing such peaceful sleep since that day and told me even his breathing has changed. He feels so calm and free, there are no words to express it thoroughly.

I thought the change was incredible in 2016, I sure wasn't ready for this new level of commitment on Phil's part. The next morning, Phil told our children of the wonderful workings of the Lord in his life and committed afresh to serve him as a father and as a family wherever He would lead us.

God was so merciful to me that August night. He clearly whispered in my heart that He would keep Satan away from me and my family for a full

8 days. No attacks, no wrong thinking, just peace. It was astonishing! If this is how heaven is going to be like, I cannot wait to get there and stand in the presence of my sweet Savior! He even sent a powerful vision to one of our sons through a dream. Many spiritual trials still lay ahead for our family, but He clearly demonstrated through the dream that if we obey His leading, the enemy will have no power over us, unless the Lord allows it personally. I hope this encourages you to follow Him all the more as it does for Phil and me.

Surgery day came early September for Sebastien and the same peace that held us through all these months carried us to face this ordeal. That morning we felt incredible strength fill our bodies as we placed our child in the hands of the cardiac nurses. Both Phil and I felt God's whisper in our hearts simultaneously. When we looked at the staff, God impressed on us that those people were His personal vessels that day and not to worry about the outcome of the surgery. Some mishaps did ensue in the two weeks after the surgery, but thankfully they were all resolved and we were able to come back home at the end of September. Sebastien was doing great considering a small opening remained in his heart that was too big for them to close up completely. We still committed to trusting our great God and peace ruled our hearts and minds as the doctors had told us there was a very real possibility for another open-heart surgery to close it up. What a surprise it was for us to learn at his last check up that the opening is completely closed up. None of the doctors have a human explanation for this, but we know it was a miracle from God!

From one who has been through many hardships in my marriage and life, hear me when I say to never lose hope. God knows exactly what you are going through and if you seek Him with all your heart, mind, soul and strength, you **WILL** find Him. When all seems broken, grab His Hand, pour your heart out to Him, He already knows how you feel.

I can assure you that now I am truly thankful for all these trials. Because if it had not been for them, I would not have met God in such deep personal ways. I do not view trials and difficulties the same way today. Anything that brings you to your knees is a good thing. In that position there is only one way to look - up to Him who made us and loves us more than we will ever know.

One song that really summarizes the change God made in me over these years is "Bring the Rain" by *Mercy Me*. As the chorus says: "*I know there will be days where this life brings me pain, but if that's what it takes to praise you Jesus, bring the rain.*"

God will never let you down, never! Now let me begin to unwrap what He taught me all these years through these trials....

"I was pushed hard, so that I was falling,
but the Lord helped me.
The Lord is my strength and my song;
He has become my salvation."

Psalm 118:13-14 (ESV)

"Surely God is my help,
the Lord is the One who sustains me."

Psalm 54:4 (NIV)

CHAPTER TWO

NO COINCIDENCES

"Take that which God has given you and share it."

Stephen F. Olford

I do not know what your life is like, what you have been through or are going through at this moment. But I know I am not the only one to have lived through hard seasons and heartbreaks in marriage. We are many. In fact, if you have been married for any period of time you have had challenging times.

I do not know where you are on your spiritual journey either, but I know there are no coincidences in this world. You picked up this book for a reason. I do not know your reason, but God does. I believe you have this book in your hands because you are looking for answers. Answers only God can give you. I wanted to share my story with you so that you would understand my passion for helping you find your answers in God. Acts 17:26-27 says :

> *"From one man He made every nation of men, that they should inhabit the whole earth; and determined the times set for them and the exact places where they should live. God did this so that men would seek Him and perhaps reach out for Him and find Him, though He is not far from each one of us." (NLT)*

This verse from the Bible says that God is not far from each one of us and that He determined the times and the places where you and I would live. He knew when you would be born, and who your parents would be. He knew that with them you would learn all the necessary things in order to seek Him.

I resented my past for such a long time, I couldn't understand why

I had the parents I did and why most of my childhood was filled with negative memories. I was disappointed that my parents didn't have a desire to raise us as a tight knit family and didn't or couldn't connect on a heart level with us. They spent most of their days either working or watching TV and didn't make the effort in getting to know me, my friends or their families. But all of these life circumstances God used to draw me to seek Him. His desire was to connect with me and He desires that same connection with you. No one else on the face of the earth knows you as intimately, everything about you inside and out, as God Himself and He still wants to have a relationship with us and shower us with His love and care. Isn't it amazing how He orchestrates everything in our lives so that we would have opportunities to seek and know Him?

The truth is God is trustworthy because He knows all about us and loves us. It is easy to trust when all is going well. But what about the bad times? How are we to trust Him for that too? In the first years of being a Christian, I wanted the quick fix option. Hard times are not pleasant. Understandably, we want out.

With every passing difficulty throughout my story, I could see I was growing and changing. My attitudes, my emotions, my behaviors were changing as I learned to trust God in the difficult times. I could see myself becoming less discouraged the more I drew closer to Him. Difficulties did not seem as hard with time, lessons learned and placing my faith in how God would lead me in the difficulties I was facing became easier. I did not have to understand all the little details of the outcomes and future because I was learning that I could trust Him completely. He would always do a much better job than all the things I tried to do to fix my life. I was learning in reality what the Bible said about faith:

> *"Trust in the Lord with all your heart*
> *and do not lean on your own understanding;*
> *In all your ways acknowledge Him,*
> *and He will make straight your paths ."*
>
> *Proverbs 3:5-6 (ESV)*

With all of your heart - not part of the way. He wants all of our hearts. Why? Because His ways are perfect even when we do not understand them.

We are not promised that we will understand how things will turn out and why they happen the way they do. Sometimes God allows us to see these things, but often He doesn't. It's not easy to accept that our lives are out of our control, but it's where we need to get in our walk of trust and faith in Him. His ways are above and so much better than our understanding. If you are sincere in your search, you will find Him. When we trust Him in every aspect of our lives and our marriages, little or big, He will do what He promises in Proverbs 3, *make your paths straight.*

"Now faith is the assurance of things hoped for,
the conviction of things not seen."

Hebrews 11:1 (ESV)

Faith is having such confidence and trust in Him that we do not doubt His good and perfect will to sustain us when life gets hard. It's knowing that whatever God chooses to do with the situation you are currently facing is His best for you. It's knowing beyond the shadow of a doubt that it will bring glory to His name. That and that alone should be our hope, not that He will use it to satisfy our own desires. That would be selfishness, which does not bring glory to our Maker. Approaching it in that way won't bring any lasting results in our marriages either. We can have hope for more than a temporary self-satisfying solution to our problems. We should hope that our marriages bring glory to God. God is the One who established the institution of marriage, and I believe that He alone knows the best way to make our marriages lasting and purposeful. Trust Him. There are no coincidences or mistakes in His plan. He is doing everything for your good and His glory.

"Marriage was not made to make us happy, it was made to make us holy"

Gary Thomas in *Sacred Marriage*

CHAPTER THREE

REMOVE THE PLANK

"The human heart is the most deceitful of all things,
and desperately wicked.
Who really knows how bad it is?
But I, the Lord, search all hearts
and examine secret motives.
I give all people their due rewards,
according to what their actions deserve."

Jeremiah 17:9-10 (NLT)

We may not see the resolution of the difficulties we are going through immediately. Sometimes, like my story, it may take years. From the time we met to the time Phil was freed from his sexual immorality and pornography addiction, it was more than 20 years. And these changes came only after I started to see that my attitude was hindering God's work in Phil. I learned that the first person I needed to look at was me.

Until we are completely honest with God and willing for Him to open our eyes as to how our attitude and our ways are hindering His work in our marriage (and life in general), we will not see much change. Our paths will not be made straight. We will only see our significant other as being the problem. Placing blame is easy, because it removes the responsibility from us. That is a lie. I knew deep down inside that my nagging and bitterness were wrong, but I refused to accept my responsibility for these sins. I excused them as normal because of how I was being treated. I wanted Phil to change without making any effort of my own. I would blame my attitude and other behaviors on his sins. I was convinced that He was ruining our relationship. It was all Phil's fault. If only he would change then everything would be good.

Hear me when I say this is a very dangerous road to be on. Your problems will only get worse and will never be fully resolved and healed if you continue to point the finger of blame at the other person. The only person you can change in this world is you. It is hard to see ourselves for who we really are, but it is the only way to true freedom. And that's where finding peace in life and in our own marriages can begin, by cooperating with God to change us.

Looking honestly at ourselves through the eyes of our Maker is really not pleasant. Our hearts can be full of selfishness, pride, and many other sins. It is not a pretty sight and hard to admit that our behaviors and words are coming from these self-focused motives. Even as my life was changing, underneath the surface, in my heart, many foes still lived: anger, bitterness, resentment, insecurity and pride. I still carried a lot of baggage from my former life, and with an unhealthy marriage as well, I was headed for trouble.

When I gave my life over to Christ on that November day of 2007, I indeed felt free from a lot of the bondage I was living in. At the same time, I did not realize how much work still needed to be done in my life. I thought that because Christ had paid for my sins, setting me free from that bondage, I was above other people. We are indeed set apart from unbelievers when we make a deliberate choice to follow Jesus, but in no way are we above others. I especially began thinking this way toward my husband.

I had accepted Christ, but gave no grace toward Phil, who was still on that journey. My pride showed itself by being critical and comparing myself to Phil. 'If Phil could only see how bad his sins were. Look how I have been saved and he is on the road to an eternal separation from God.' Because of this attitude, I would correct him, but not always in a very loving manner. I believed that if he could only change and see the damage he was causing both of us, all would be better.

That's what pride does, it keeps you from seeing your own part in the relationship. My prideful attitude was destroying our relationship and I couldn't see it because I was focused on Phil's imperfections. I was constantly comparing my "good deeds" with Phil's "bad deeds." I was the one taking care of the kids, homeschooling them, pointing them to Jesus, cooking, cleaning, running most errands and paying the bills. Wasn't I justified to harbor some kind of anger toward Phil? He even called himself a Christian, but never read his Bible, lived a worldly life from Sunday afternoon to the next Sunday morning. He was the one with the lust issues, the pornography addiction, the adultery and he was the one living out of God's will. Rarely would I ever think something positive about him. Almost never would I offer a compliment for helping me. His sins were way bigger than mine I thought. Wasn't I justified? I was so much holier than that! He was the one causing so much pain and problems in our marriage.

And so it continued round and round in my heart and mind. I justified my "little" sins of anger and unforgiveness. I convinced myself it wouldn't really matter in the end. I was pretty sure I could explain it all to God once I saw Him. I was planning on getting baptized and making my public declaration of faith. Surely that was more than enough to convince God of my genuineness in following Him. Surely the Lord would accept my complaints and see how utterly miserable Phil was making me and the children. He would be on my side.

I want to assure you that I am in no way invalidating how difficult it is to live through adultery and other sexual sins committed against us. It is heartbreaking and devastating. I get that. The danger is to let pride turn to anger and sink deep into our hearts and souls and make us resentful and bitter. In my situation, my pride overtook my heart, affecting what I believed, and my behavior followed. The Lord is the only one that can keep our hearts from going down that destructive path.

Having no Christian family and no godly mature people in my life at that time also kept me from realizing what I was doing. No one was there to teach me that I needed "heart surgery" to change the things I was believing that were lies. Beliefs about myself, my husband, my marriage, my life. One of the dangers in leaving our hearts to "go their own way" is the hindrance of growth in our spiritual life. I would get stuck and couldn't seem to grow past a certain point. I believe this was because I was refusing God access to the important parts of my life - my heart, my thoughts and the true motives that led me down that road. And to be honest, deep down I still wanted to keep the sinful control over those areas of my life.

Our sins will not be as obvious as our spouse's sins since it's always easier to see other people's shortcomings before our own. If left unconfessed, those sins become a plank in our own eyes, leaving us blind and unable to grow spiritually or change. We need God to show us what needs to be removed from our own hearts and eyes before we even begin to hope for change in our mates. When our hearts remain unchecked, our attitudes and our thinking will be centered on ourselves and our own desires.

Just like it only takes a single apple to rot all the other apples in the bag, it only takes one unchecked heart and unconfessed sins to rot our marriages. Until our hearts are cleansed from all unrighteousness and fully open to God, change in our marriages will not be lasting. Repentance is crucial in all aspects of our lives. Otherwise our sins will become planks in our eyes and walls in our hearts that block the Spirit's work in us. We will miss God's blessings for our lives and our marriages.

If we were to turn the tables and we were the one causing major pain and heartache in someone else's life, how would we like that person to respond to us? This is a good question to ask to help us discern our part and our next steps in any relationship. When I was faced with this question in my own life it was another turning point for me. Of course, I would want another person to extend grace, mercy, love, patience and understanding to me if I hurt them. Who would want to be accused with venomous words, being torn apart emotionally and left alone? And yet I was doing this very thing to my husband. This response would be even more appreciated if I carried guilt and shame from sinful addictions.

Since this, and more, is what Jesus offers us if we turn to Him and repent, I had to ask myself, as a believer, why I wasn't offering the same forgiveness and grace that was given to me, to my husband. The pride I felt for the position and perfection and suffering and sacrifice I held over my husband was holding me back from responding correctly to him. Me, the Christian, was the one lacking love, grace, mercy, patience and understanding with my 'poor me' attitude. I was poor. Poor in the things I needed most to forgive and love my husband the way God wanted me to.

"Actions must follow what one believes,
else no one could claim to believe it."

Dietrich Bonhoeffer

Your husband might still be an adulterer, like mine was, or he might still be addicted to pornography or be committing many other hurtful sins, but we desperately need to make sure that for our part we are right with God. Sin is sin in God's eyes. If I claim to be a Christian I must follow through with the things I believe I am called to do, even when life is hard. The first step in restoring my marriage needed to begin with me. Jesus said we would have trouble in this world. But He also promised that He had overcome the world (John 16:33). God also assures us that His grace is sufficient for us (2 Corinthians 12:9). Nothing and no one else except God Almighty can or will help you through your trials and difficulties in life and in your marriage. He alone can help you remove that plank in your eye and help you see what you need to do, with His help, to rebuild your marriage.

"Trust Him at all times, O people; pour out your hearts to Him, for God is our refuge."

Psalm 62:8 (NIV)

"If I had not confessed the sin in my heart, the Lord would not have listened. But God did listen! He paid attention to my prayer. Praise God, who did not ignore my prayer or withdraw His unfailing love from me."

Psalm 66:18-20 (NLT)

It is so much easier to navigate our Christian lives when we allow Him to know us and reveal ourselves inside and out. I know He doesn't need us to tell Him anything about what we are like since He already knows, but we need to tell Him for our own healing journey. There is nothing more freeing than admitting all of our shortcomings and trusting God to make us the person He wants us to be, because only then can He begin to really work in us. Only then are our hearts open for Him to work out His ways. When we "come clean" with our sins He can forgive us. We have nothing to lose, only forgiveness and freedom to gain if we are open for His Holy Spirit to minister to us. If this book has been put in your hands and you are being prompted by God to do something, I urge you to not hold back on the call of God over your life. If you have never trusted Jesus as your Savior and turned your life over to Him, my prayer for you is that you will give your whole life to Him. To the One who made you and knows you. To the One who sent His One and only Son to die on the cross in order to redeem you. Jesus' blood was sufficient to pay for all your sins, even the ones you are ashamed to admit are destroying your marriage or that you are still struggling with after years of being a Christian. He willingly stretched out His arms on the cross for all of those. Now is the time to decide what you will do. Will you trust Him with your life?

"If we confess our sins, he is faithful and just to forgive us our sins and to cleanse us from all unrighteousness."

1 John 1:9 (ESV)

If you have already trusted Jesus to be your Savior and you have been struggling in your life and marriage, I would urge you right now to ask Our Heavenly Father what areas of your life need to be uncovered and given over to Him. Then let Him enter your most secret thoughts and give Him all your broken emotions, your hurts, your concerns, your failures - all those things He shows you to give to Him. I completely understand that this can be very hard, but a full repentance is needed so our guilt and shame can be dealt with. And once those have been removed, my friend, we get to experience our Lord in ways we never did before. We become vessels for Him to work in and through us, pointing others to Him, ministering to others, starting with our own spouses.

"Search me, O God, and know my heart;
test me and know my anxious thoughts.
Point out anything in me that offends you,
and lead me along the path of everlasting life."

Psalm 139:23-24 (NLT)

Our attitudes will change to reflect His. His love will become ours to share with difficult people including our difficult spouses. He will lift our discouragement and hopelessness and we will have assurance that He will carry us through whatever season or difficulty we are in. All these things will not happen overnight, but as He transforms you from the inside out it will be worth all of the effort and time and pain spent to be free from the things that are holding you back from moving forward in your spiritual life and your relationships.

When I saw my own shortcomings and sins and acknowledged my need for God's help in my life, my heart finally had room for His transformation. The moment God impressed Romans 3:23 on my heart, as I was complaining to Him about all the wrong things Phil was doing to ruin our marriage, was when I realized my pride and sinfulness was a wall between Phil and Him. The first thing that began to change was my attitude toward my husband.

Did Phil change? No, I did. When I allowed God access to my heart and turned everything over to Him I was then able to see the positive things about my husband, and that I shared the responsibility for our problems. I thank God that He opened my eyes and helped me remove the plank in my own eye instead of focusing on the speck in my husband's!

"You hypocrite,
first take the plank out of your own eye,
and then you will see clearly
to remove the speck from your brother's eye."

Matthew 7:5 (NIV)

CHAPTER FOUR

HOPE AND HELP FOR THE JOURNEY

"And I am certain that God,
who began the good work within you,
will continue his work until it is finally finished
on the day when Christ Jesus returns."

Philippians 1:6 (NLT)

I understand how hard all this might be to read if you have been wounded by your husband and if it is ongoing. I have been there. Days where your heart is shattered into pieces. Days where you wonder if there is any hope of change. Days where you feel surrounded by a thick fog and just getting through the day is challenging. Remembering some of those days still brings tears to my eyes. I understand exactly how that feels and it is a very difficult place to be.

But God assures us that with Him, all things are possible (John 14:14, Matthew 19:26, Mark 9:23). In those hard moments, we need to cling to His promises. He is unchanging. Circumstances can change in the blink of an eye, but not our God (Hebrews 13:8). What He says He will do. When we give Him our shattered, broken hearts He knows how to put the pieces back together again.

As I write this, it has been over a year since Phil's complete repentance. And even though I am doing so much better, some pieces of my heart need further healing. But as I trust God, He has shown me that I can keep trusting Him with these issues. He has not abandoned Phil, on the contrary, He will keep working on him. And He has not abandoned me. I am a work in progress and so is my husband. With that perspective in mind, I can keep living out my faith, resting in the assurance that God still has our marriage very much in His very capable hands.

We all have different temptations that come our way, often depending on our past struggles and sins. Lust of the eyes is one temptation Phil will need to be watchful for the rest of his life. Mine is to express my feelings without going to God first, thus letting them come out with no filter. I had to learn a great deal about taming my tongue and working out my issues with God first before I shared my feelings with my husband, which could create another issue if those feelings were wrongly expressed. I am in no way trying to justify our husbands' sins. Not one bit. Neither am I justifying my own sins because of my past. What I am trying to convey is that perfection is no longer part of this world since Adam and Eve sinned. We will continue to struggle against our sinful nature until we get to heaven. But we do have a choice.

Lysa Terkeurst paints a beautiful imagery of our condition in her book *It's Not Supposed to be This Way*. One of the messages she conveys in her book is that we live between two gardens. The garden of Eden, where perfection was created and broken and the New Heaven God will bring after the end times. And in between these two gardens, life is hard and filled with brokenness. Our hope of surviving life successfully *between two gardens* is to cling to Our Maker. Only He can fill our hearts and minds with a peace that surpasses all understanding (Phil 4:7), only He can heal our brokenness and rid us of sin. Life *between two gardens* without Him will be void of healing.

I wondered at times if I would ever fully heal from my brokenness. Amazingly, the more time went by, the more I became convinced that although I want to continue to be healed I don't want to lose the memory of the pain and hurt I've experienced. Let me explain. In the spring of 2019, Phil and I gave our marriage testimony at our church. In the following weeks I met with women who were going through hard seasons in their marriages. I could completely relate to them and my heart broke for them as I began praying for these women. I then asked God if He could not completely heal my pain. I wanted to be able to have compassion and feel the pain these women were experiencing so that I could carry their burdens with them and minister to them as God would lead me. None of our struggles are wasted in God's Kingdom. He can use your pain in order to help someone else down the road. His plans far outweigh anything we could ever imagine.

God loves us too much to give our lives and marriages a quick fix. He desires for us to look more and more like His Son Jesus Christ, not for us to get a fairy-tale ending. There are lots of pleasurable moments in marriage, but to obtain true oneness will often require going through trials and difficulties. These will come and go, sanding away our imperfections if we let them.

"No marriage arrives at a beautiful, stable place without pain."

Charles Price, *Gender and Sexuality study*

The times I learned the most were in the valleys of life. As Christians, that is where our faith is tested. Will we trust God with the outcome or will we turn to ourselves and worldly attempts in order to navigate our way? With time, trials and difficulties have a way of refining us. Though not pleasant, they are very necessary. These God-ordained times will help us wash away the sins that so easily entangle us and keep us from moving forward. His holy goal is to prepare us for the Day of Jesus Christ. On that Day, I can guarantee that you and I will not be thinking of all those marital issues anymore. We will enter His presence with rejoicing. Our tears will be wiped away and our sadness turned into joy!

As we wait for that Day, what should we do in these days to navigate the difficulties and hurts? First of all, I would suggest you find an older, trustworthy godly woman in whom you can confide. Two are better than one (Ecclesiastes 4:9-10). And since that person is outside of your circumstances, she can give you objective advice and pray for you consistently and meaningfully. If you cannot think of a specific person, ask someone at your church if they could recommend an older woman to you.

Second, you could join a prayer group or a woman's Bible study group and find trustworthy people who could help carry your burden, come alongside you and pray for your marriage. Be careful that you do not use this time to speak badly of your husband in public though, as this will cause the Lord to remove His hand of blessing from you. You will be tearing down your marriage by disgracing your husband.

And, third, there is the option of meeting with one of your pastors or a qualified Christian counselor to help you walk through this journey of healing. Meeting together as a couple is best if it is possible, but if your husband isn't willing at the moment, continue to pray for him and get help for your own issues so you can respond to him in a godly way.

If none of these options are possible, remember that first and foremost, you are never alone. God is always by your side (Hebrews 13:5b, Jesus in Matthew 28:20). You can cry out to Him and be assured He will hear you. And even with these suggestions mentioned, God, through the Holy Spirit, is our best Help and our Comforter in times of trouble (see verses below). He should actually be the first person we go to. By relying on Him first, we allow Him to guide us through those hard seasons and to lead us to the help we need. He is the only person who will never let you down, judge you based on your emotions or failures, or forget about you. People will fall short, but God is all powerful, all knowing, and always present.

So hope is first found in Him, and then others who follow Him. I know some trials can seem to go on so very long, but do not lose hope. When you reach out to God, He will carry you through even the most difficult and trying times. You are not alone. He knows.

After you have come through these trials, looking back you will see His provision all of the way. Though we cannot control how our husbands will respond to the Lord's promptings and discipline, we know the Lord loves us and no matter what happens, He will not give up on us. So Sister, don't give up! YOU are loved much more than you can ever imagine!

I want to add here that if your situation is life threatening or dangerous, please seek professional help and, if needed, find a way to temporarily remove yourself from that situation until you can find the appropriate help for your marriage and for yourself.

Scriptures on hope and comfort:

See: Deuteronomy 31:8-9; Joshua 1:9-10; Psalm 9:9; Psalm 23; Psalm 27:1; Psalm 46:1; Psalm 86:17; Psalm 116:1-2; Psalm 119:48-52; Psalm 119:76; Lamentations 3:31-62; John 14:16-17, 26-27.

The Scriptures are such an amazing comfort to our souls. Why not write one or more of these verses on an index card, in your journal or

CHAPTER FIVE

FINDING STRENGTH FOR THE JOURNEY

*"Our intimacy with God
is His highest priority for our lives
because it determines the impact of our lives.
The more profound our fellowship with the Father,
the more powerful our lives -
regardless of whether we're educated, attractive,
wealthy, or of a prominent social standing.
We don't have to be perfect, not by any means.
No, it is our relationship with God that makes all the difference in our lives -
our love for Him, our willingness to serve Him,
and our dependence upon His Holy Spirit."*

Charles F. Stanley in *Courageous Faith*

In God I have found the One and Only who will never leave me and who will always love me. And I have come to understand that He deserves first place in my life. I love my husband very much, but Phil cannot offer me what God can. Phil cannot perfectly love me, he cannot give me peace of mind and heart, and he certainly cannot heal me or guide me perfectly. Only God can do that.

For many years I had idolized my marriage relationship over my relationship with God. I was trying to find fulfillment in my marriage before seeking true fulfillment with God. Our acceptance is in God because Jesus accomplished that on the cross. Our identity is in Christ (see verses at the end of chapter), and our future is sealed with God (2 Corinthians 1:22). Marriage is one means to get to know God more deeply, to grow more like Christ, and to be an example of the relationship between Jesus and His church to those around us.

Our final acceptance, our final identity, and our future are found only in God and His Son Jesus Christ. No marriage can ever give us that. But God can. And He gives us practical ways to build strength in our personal lives that will impact our relationships. Some of these helps are His Word, prayer and the Holy Spirit.

Charles Stanley (quoted above) is one of the people God has used to point me to Jesus so He could remold me in His image. I love that quote because it assures me that I do not need to be perfect. God takes us where we are, like we are and remolds the clay of our lives into a vessel that can be used by Him to reach and minister to others. Books from Christian authors like Dr. Stanley were where I gained strength to go through my trials and difficulties. But nothing gave me more strength than the Word of God itself.

> *"Oh, the joys of those who do not follow the advice of the wicked,*
> *or stand around with sinners, or join in with mockers.*
> **But they delight in the law of the LORD,**
> **meditating on it <u>day and night</u>.**
> *They are like trees planted along the riverbank, bearing fruit each season.*
> *Their leaves never wither, and they prosper in all they do."*
>
> *Psalm 1:1-3 (NLT, emphasis mine)*

Since we cannot talk to God face to face, His Word is where we go to get to know Him and His will for our lives. After reading the Scriptures, I always feel much more prepared to face the day ahead of me. It did not happen overnight though. I had lots of questions as I began to seriously study the Word. *How did that passage apply to me? What was the context of those verses? How can I apply this in my own life?* And over and over again, He would lead me to the answers in His Word:

> *"**Teach me** your decrees, O LORD;*
> *I will keep them to the end.*
> ***Give me understanding** and I will obey your instructions;*
> *I will put them into practice with all my heart.*
> ***Make me walk** along the path of your commands,*
> *for that is where my happiness is found.*

> ***Give me an eagerness for your law***
> *rather than a love for money!*
> ***Turn my eyes from worthless things,***
> *and give me life through your word.*
> ***Reassure me of your promise,***
> *made to those who fear you.*
> ***Help me*** *abandon my shameful ways;*
> *for your regulations are good.*
> ***I long to obey your commandments!***
> *Renew my life with your goodness."*

Psalm 119:33-40 (NLT, emphasis mine)

God's Word is the well of strength for the believer. The thirstier I got for His help and guidance, the more passionate I became in studying His Word. I wanted Him to guide me. I wanted to do more than just read and learn verses. I wanted to understand, to be able to apply those concepts, and know His purpose for my life. I got to the point that the more time I spent in His presence, I did not feel like leaving that presence. I wanted Him in every aspect of my life. And He honored my desire for Him by meeting me in His Word and teaching me how to live a life that pleases Him through His Word.

Prayer is another tool God has given to us to strengthen us on our journey. Through very intimate, personal times of prayer, we can pour our hearts out, express our true emotions, and ask for healing, help and guidance. There is nothing we cannot share with God that He does not already know. We can open up in the presence of the Almighty and pour our hearts out to Him. No questions or concerns are beyond His scope. Nothing is too small or too insignificant for Him who knit us together in our mother's womb (Psalm 139:13-16). He knows us better than any human being can know us. We can come assured, confident and boldly into His presence. Spending time with Him through those intimate conversations will change, shape and strengthen you.

My own experiences testify to this. When I did not know where to turn for answers and I was full of hurt and pain, I drew closer to the Lord through prayer. Although very intense at times, I didn't hide anything from Him. My hurts, my anger, my frustration, my tears, my selfish motives - He listened every time as I poured out my heart to Him. Through all of this, and with time, I felt much stronger from having spent those precious moments alone in His presence. Prayer carried me through some of the worst days where I felt very downcast and alone. There are no words that can express the incredible closeness and love I experienced. If you ever doubted that God listens to you, I can testify that He hears you - always. Ask Him to reveal Himself to you, to show you how much you are loved and precious in His eyes. He will.

Many people believe they must fix themselves before they come to God. This isn't true. He wants to spend time with you. He wants to hear your heart. Be authentic. Be honest. Tell Him exactly what is on your mind and in your heart. Then watch Him work through you and in your situation. He holds the future in His hands, so only He can direct you (1 Peter 1:3-4, 2 Corinthians 4:17-18, Romans 8:18-25). Don't think that because He hears you this means you can expect to get your own way. We must not tell Him what He should be doing with our lives. We are in no position to tell the Creator how to manage His creation. We must come humbly to Him in faith. It is not easy, but it is so worth it to be freed from the bondage in our lives and to receive the growth we so earnestly want. Hebrews 11:6 says, *"Faith is the assurance of things unseen."* Unseen. That's why it's called faith. We have no idea what or how God will work in our lives, but by faith we do not doubt His love for us and His perfect plan for our lives. For better OR for worse.

> *"For my thoughts are not your thoughts,*
> *neither are your ways my ways, declares the Lord.*
> *As the heavens are higher than the earth,*
> *so are my ways higher than your ways*
> *and my thoughts than your thoughts."*
>
> Isaiah 55:8-9 (NIV)

Not only do we have His Word and the privilege of prayer but we have the Holy Spirit living inside us to help us live lives pleasing to Him. Before Jesus ascended to heaven, He promised the disciples that God would send them help. That help came in the form of God's Holy Spirit on the Day of Pentecost. And it radically transformed each and every one of the disciples.

They became bold in their witness for Christ. They became fearless and willing to die for the cause of Christ to proclaim His Name to all. This is the power that resides in us when we believe in our Lord and Savior Jesus Christ. He sends us the Holy Spirit to enable us to walk in accordance with His will and to become more and more of a reflection of His Son. Our part is to allow the Spirit to transform us. As we submit our lives to the Holy Spirit and allow Him to control our lives day by day and moment by moment, He will faithfully transform us into the likeness of Jesus.

The Holy Spirit will not only grow godly fruit in us (Galatians 5:22-23, 1 Corinthians 13:4-8, 2 Peter 1:5-7), but He will be our very present help in understanding the Word of God - specifically how it will speak to us in our situation. He will help us when we have no idea what to pray (Romans 8:26). He can redirect us when we are straying off the path with our attitudes and actions. He can help us see where we need to change and submit our wills to His will.

Along with all these helps that the Lord gives to strengthen us on this journey we need to remember that the Christian walk is one of patience and step by step learning. Because of our sin nature, we tend to resort to our human flesh faster than run to God. Early on in my journey I often felt like I was taking two steps forward and three steps backward. And I would get angry with myself. I did not hide those sentiments from God, I was honest with my frustration and with time I learned to not react so quickly. Slowly but surely, I grew to take two steps forward and one step backward. I was encouraged by the work He was doing in my life during these times. It's similar to when a child starts walking. He doesn't just get up and walk. It takes multiple tries of falling, getting up, falling, getting up, and falling and getting up again. Spiritual growth is much the same way. We need to be patient with ourselves and allow God to shape and mold us through His Word, prayer and His Spirit. Lasting change, maturity and wisdom do not happen overnight. So do not put more pressure on yourself than God does.

We will never reach perfection on this side of life (Philippians 1:6). We will keep making mistakes, and that's okay. The important thing is that we keep moving forward in growth and godly attitudes. Stay humble and teachable. Be willing to quickly recognize your wrongs and kill your pride. Forgive quickly and look at others the same way Jesus does. God will honor your every effort to draw near Him and obey Him. And little by little, if you persevere, He will change you, your marriage, your family, and every relationship around you. Your dependence upon Him will have ripple effects in every area of your life. With the Lord's help, you will grow in wisdom and strength, and your relationships will bring honor and glory to Him.

Get out there, Sisters! Reach out to God with all your heart and soul, spend time in His presence, and then watch Him move in your circumstances and relationships!

Scriptures on prayer:

See: 1 Chronicles 16:11; 2 Chronicles 6:21; Job 22:27; Psalm 4:1; Psalm 17:6; Psalm 102:1; Psalm 119:148; Proverbs 15:29; Jeremiah 29:12; Matthew 5:44; Matthew 6:7, 9-13; Matthew 26:41; Mark 11:24; Luke 11:2-4; Luke 18:1; Ephesians 6:18; Philippians 4:6-7; Colossians 4:2; 1 Thessalonians 5:17.

Scriptures about meditating on the Word of God:

See: Joshua 1:8; Psalm 1; Psalm 19:14; Psalm 119:15, 78b, 97-99, 148; Psalm 143:5; Proverbs 4:20-22; 1 Timothy 4:13-15.

As we mentioned in the last chapter, write them down, hide them in your heart and they will give you strength when you will need it.

"God is our refuge and strength,
always ready to help in times of trouble"

Psalm 46:1 (NLT).

CHAPTER SIX

LAYING DOWN OUR LIVES

"And so, dear brothers and sisters,
I plead with you to give your bodies to God
because of all he has done for you.
Let them be a living and holy sacrifice—
the kind he will find acceptable.
This is truly the way to worship him.
Don't copy the behavior and customs of this world,
but let God transform you into a new person by changing the way you think.
Then you will learn to know God's will for you,
which is good and pleasing and perfect."

Romans 12: 1-2 (NLT)

If you have made it this far with me, I am more than grateful for your perseverance! On this journey God will reward your every step. You are on the path to victory. I am conscious that all we have talked about up to this point is hard, perhaps very hard, but hopefully you are starting to feel less discouraged and freer than when you started reading this book. I trust that you have truly begun to realize that you cannot change anyone but yourself. What our spouses choose to do with their lives will affect us on more than one level, but the reverse is also true. What we choose to do with our lives can affect them on more than one level.

Another hurdle to restoring our hearts and minds with the goal of healthy relationships is laying down our lives. This is possibly the hardest thing we have talked about so far. This is not a promise of guaranteed marital success. I could never affirm such a thing. But in order to live our lives according to the will of God, it is necessary to understand what it means to lay down our lives. So what does laying down our lives really mean or look like for you and me? Since I am not a Bible scholar or an expert on the topic, I turned to the Scriptures to find some answers:

"This is how we know what love is: Jesus Christ laid down His life for us. And we ought to lay down our lives for our brothers."

1 John 3:16 (NIV)

*"Then he (Jesus) said to the crowd, "If any of you wants to be my follower, you **must** give up your own way, take up your cross **daily**, and follow me. If you try to hang on to your life, you will lose it. But if you give up your life for my sake, you will save it. And what do you benefit if you gain the whole world but are yourself lost or destroyed?"*

Luke 9:23-25 (NLT, emphasis and parenthesis mine)

*"If you refuse to take up your cross and follow me, you are **not worthy of being mine**"*

Matthew 10:38 (NLT, emphasis mine)

Those verses still have a profound impact on me today. And every time I read them, I have to ask myself if I have indeed lost my life and picked up my cross in a manner that is worthy of Christ. Laying down our lives means we are willing to surrender our desires and our wills for what God wills and picking up our cross means we are willing to accept the hardship and suffering that may come from following Jesus.

Notice that this kind of attitude is a daily attitude. Every day, we have to choose to lose our lives and pick up our crosses. Otherwise we are NOT worthy of Jesus. Ouch! Talk about a sting. No wonder Jesus tells us to count the cost before we make a decision to follow Him. Following Him requires sacrifice.

"And if you do not carry your own cross and follow me, you cannot be my disciple. But don't begin until you count the cost. For who would begin construction of a building without first calculating the cost to see if there is enough money to finish it?

*Otherwise, you might complete only the foundation
before running out of money,
and then everyone would laugh at you.
They would say, 'There's the person who started that building
and couldn't afford to finish it!'
Or what king would go to war against another king
without first sitting down with his counselors
to discuss whether his army of 10,000
could defeat the 20,000 soldiers marching against him?
And if he can't, he will send a delegation to discuss terms of peace
while the enemy is still far away.*
**So you cannot become my disciple without
giving up everything you own."**

Luke 14: 27-33 (NLT, emphasis mine)

*"Jesus replied: No one who puts his hand to the plow
and looks back is fit for service in the Kingdom of God."*

Luke 9:62 (NIV)

John MacArthur plainly explains this in his book *The Gospel According to Jesus:*

"When Jesus called people to follow Him, He was not seeking companions to be His sidekicks or admirers whom He could entertain with miracles. He was calling people to yield completely and unreservedly to His Lordship."

Completely and unreservedly. Keeping nothing for ourselves, but laying all down at His feet for His Kingdom purposes. All the brokenness surrounding our lives and our marriages, our unbelieving or difficult spouses, and not looking back with regrets about choosing Jesus over our own ideals. John MacArthur continues:

"A true believer is one who signs up for life. The bumper-sticker sentiment "Try Jesus" is a mentality foreign to real discipleship - Faith is not an experiment, but a lifelong commitment. It means taking up the cross daily, giving all for Christ each day. It means no reservations, no uncertainty, no hesitation

(Luke 9:59-61). It means nothing is knowingly held back, nothing purposely shielded from His Lordship, nothing stubbornly kept from His control. It calls for painful severing of the tie with the world, a sealing of the escape hatches, a ridding oneself of any kind of security to fall back on in case of failure. Genuine believers know they are going ahead with Christ until death. Having put their hand to the plow, they will not look back (Luke 9:62)."

No reservations, no uncertainty about who comes first, no hesitation to make Him first. It means nothing is knowingly held back - even our attitude towards our marriages and our spouses when all turns out wrong. Nothing is purposely shielded from His Lordship - not even our hearts and thoughts. Nothing is stubbornly kept from His control - not our pride, anger, resentment, attitude or bitterness. It calls for *painful* severing of the tie with the world - going God's way and not my way. A sealing of the escape hatches - not running for temporary pleasure or modes of escapism when difficulties arise. A ridding oneself *of any kind of security to fall back on in case of failure* - not holding to a false sense of security that my marriage is my life, but willingly offering Him all the aspects of my marriage whether they succeed or fail, whether my spouse repents or not. Having put their hand to the plow, they will NOT look back.

This is what laying down our lives means. It is *for life*, for better or for worse. When Job was struck with innumerable, successive catastrophes and his wife told him to curse God and die, he did not do such a thing. But instead he replied that if we accept good from God, we should also accept trouble from Him as well (Job 2:9-10).

Before I started writing this book, I had to ask myself if I could be kept accountable to all the words that were going to be put on paper. Obviously, if I would tell you I keep all those words perfectly, I would be lying to you and be an incredible hypocrite. I don't. I still sin and have to ask forgiveness for those times. I have to refocus my attention at times. Sin will be part of our lives until we either die or are taken up to heaven (Romans 7:21-25). If our greatest desire is to follow Christ and be at the center of God's will for our lives, then the rest of our lives will become easier to manage daily as we continue to battle sin (Romans 8:12-17) with the help of the Holy Spirit.

The apostle Paul understood well this principle of laying down his life for Christ's cause. He knew that in and of himself he could not do anything of lasting value (John 15:5-9). Only when we depend on God to be our strength can we fully experience the richness of life as it was meant to be. This is what it means to be under the Lordship of Christ. He gets first place, and through the Holy Spirit, He imparts His strength and grace into our lives so we can live to please Him.

> *"But He (Jesus) said to me, "My grace is sufficient for you,*
> *for my power is made perfect in weakness"*
> *Therefore I will boast all the more gladly about my weaknesses,*
> *so that Christ's power may rest on me.*
> *That is why, for Christ's sake, I delight in weaknesses, in insults,*
> *in hardships, in persecutions, in difficulties.*
> *For when I am weak, then I am strong."*
>
> *2 Corinthians 12: 9-10 (NIV, parenthesis mine)*

Grace is a gift we do not deserve. Dietrich Bonhoeffer in *The Cost of Discipleship* explains:

"Such grace is costly because it calls us to follow, and it is grace because it calls us to follow Jesus Christ. It is costly because it costs a man his life, and it is grace because it gives a man the only true life. It is costly because it condemns sin, and grace because it justifies the sinner. Above all, it is costly because it cost God the life of his Son:"ye were bought at a price," and what has cost God much cannot be cheap for us."

Marriage is only one aspect of our lives, but should not be our main focus. If any lasting changes are to occur, God has to be our main focus, and daily. A strong, healthy relationship with Him will ripple out in our marriages as well. Too often, we place our marriages on top of the life pyramid. We assume that if we are happy and fulfilled in that relationship that all the rest will run smoothly. Having a great marriage is a wonderful blessing, but it was never intended to replace our relationship with our Maker who must have first place in our lives. When we give our marriages first place, or any other relationship for that matter, we are telling God He is second best.

*"Many of us are missing something in life
because we are after the second best."*

Eric Lidell

By reading and meditating on the Word of God, combined with great books from godly and mature people, I have come to know and understand what it really means to lay down my life, to give Jesus lordship over my life. This is what you and I have to decide at the beginning of every new day. Choose and follow. Follow and obey. No matter what the circumstances of our life are like. Laying down our lives, dying to ourselves, our wants, our desires, and taking up our crosses, in our daily callings in obedience to Him, is one key to having a marriage that honors the Lord. And then there is Jesus. He is the best example of this sacrifice. Jesus Himself willingly offered His life for our sake. If the Son of God was willing to lose His life and come to earth for our benefit, taking our place on the cross of Calvary, don't we owe Him the same loyalty and love by giving up our right to our own life?

*"Though He was God,
He did not think of equality with God
as something to cling to.
Instead, He gave up his divine privileges;
He took the humble position of a slave
and was born as a human being.
When He appeared in human form,
He humbled Himself in obedience to God
and died a criminal death on a cross."*

Philippians 2:6-8 (NLT)

One of the things that makes laying down our lives at the feet of our Savior so hard is that not only does it mean we must turn our focus away from having what we want, but also we don't know what the outcome will be. Trusting Him with loving blindness that whatever He chooses to do with our lives will ultimately be for our good (Romans 8:28), and for His glory, is necessary when we lay down our lives. It will require us to trust Him and obey Him when we do not feel like it. Obedience and trust are ways to show the Lord our love and dedication. We cannot lay down our lives and pick and choose which commands or principles we will follow. That is still taking control of our lives. No good fruit will grow from that type of attitude, only rotten fruit, because it will not come out of a relationship with the Son of God (John 15:4-6), but from the world. Being obedient to Christ's commands will prove itself successful in every area of your life.

"Because Jesus is the Christ, He has the authority to call and to demand obedience to His Word. Jesus summons men to follow Him, not as a teacher or a pattern of the good life, but as the Christ, the Son of God"

Dietrich Bonhoeffer in *The Cost of Discipleship*

"You cannot and should not forget that obedience to the Father has been and continues to be costly and will always require great courage from us."

Charles Stanley in *Courageous Faith*

Laying down your life will require great courage, because at times it will go against the grain of our fallen nature, it will go against all the messages that are thrown at us in this world, and it may leave you standing for Christ alone in your family or marriage. But you will not be truly alone, as God will be with you and He will reward you for your faithfulness to Him.

With the help of our Lord and Savior all things are possible. Spend time in His presence and His Word as much as you can so He can give you the strength to find that sought for courage we all lack, but so desperately need. The courage to withstand all for His Name no matter what the cost. Continue to seek Him and trust Him and He will shape you into the image of Jesus.

Many people, who I have only met in books, have encouraged me in this process and on this journey. Some of them I've mentioned here in these chapters. I've prepared a list of resources at the end of the book for your benefit. I found these writings and stories encouraging and insightful. It was particularly helpful to read stories from people who laid down their lives for the cause of Christ at great cost. It helped me understand trials and difficulties in a different light and my marital issues paled in comparison to what they had gone through. They were and still are a great encouragement in my walk with God.

"Therefore, since we are surrounded
by such a great cloud of witnesses,
let us throw of everything that hinders
and the sin that so easily entangles,
and let us run with perseverance
the race marked out for us,
fixing our eyes on Jesus,
the author and perfecter of our faith,
who for the joy set before him endured the cross,
scorning its shame,
and sat down at the right hand of the throne of God.
Consider him who endured such opposition
from sinful men,
so that you will not grow weary and lose heart."

Hebrews 12 : 1-3 (NIV)

CHAPTER SEVEN

WHY IS THIS SO HARD? PART ONE: THE SINFUL NATURE

Part One: The Sinful Nature

*"Not a single person on earth is always good
and never sins."*

Ecclesiastes 7:20 (NLT)

Two of the main reasons we struggle in this life as Christians are our sinful nature and Satan, God's enemy. Let us begin with the first one. The book of Romans is a great place to study the concept of the sinful nature:

*"When Adam sinned, sin entered the world.
Adam's sin brought death,
so death spread to everyone, for everyone sinned [..]
But even greater is God's wonderful grace
and His gift of forgiveness to many through this other man, Jesus Christ.
And the result of God's gracious gift is very different
from the result of that one man's sin.
For Adam's sin led to condemnation,
but God's free gift leads to our being made right with God,
even though we are guilty of many sins."*

Romans 5:12, 15b-16 (NLT)

We see from these verses that because of Adam's sin we are all sinners from birth. The human race, and that means individually as well, is at war against the sin that our souls have struggled with since the fall of Adam and Eve.

> *"I have discovered this principle of life -*
> *that when I want to do what is right,*
> *I inevitably do what is wrong.*
> *I love God's law with all my heart.*
> *But there is another power within me*
> *that is at war with my mind.*
> *This power makes me a slave to the sin*
> *that is still within me.*
> *Oh, what a miserable person I am!*
> *Who will free me from this life that is dominated by sin and death?*
> *Thank God!*
> *The answer is in Jesus Christ our Lord."*
>
> *Romans 7:21-25 (NLT)*

We know that we are in a war and we know in the end we win because Jesus has already conquered sin and death, but then how do we live now with this sinful nature? How do we handle the sinful desires, attitudes and actions in our everyday lives?

If we are to defeat sin and live in victory over our sinful natures we must see ourselves as we truly are in Christ.

> *"Since we have been united with Him in His death,*
> *we will also be raised to life as He was.*
> *We know that our old sinful selves*
> *were crucified with Christ*
> *so that sin may lose its power in our lives.*
> *We are no longer slaves to sin.*
> *For when we died with Christ we were set free from the power of sin [..]*
> *When He died, He died once to break the power of sin.*
> *But now that He lives, He lives for the glory of God.*
> *So you should* **consider yourselves to** *be dead*
> *to the power of sin*
> *and alive to God through Christ Jesus.*

__Do not let__ sin control the way you live,
__do not give in__ to sinful desires.
__Do not let__ any part of your body become
an instrument of evil to serve sin.
Instead __give yourselves__ completely to God,
for you were dead, but now have new life.
So __use__ your whole body as an instrument
to __do__ what is right for the glory of God."
Therefore, brothers and sisters,
you have no obligation to do what your sinful nature urges you to do."

Romans 6:5-7, 10-13; Romans 8:12 (NLT, emphasis mine)

"My old self has been crucified with Christ.
It is no longer I who live, but Christ lives in me.
So I live in this earthly body by trusting in the Son of God,
who loved me and gave Himself for me."

Galatians 2:20 (NLT)

We can see from these bolded verses that sin no longer needs to control our lives. It doesn't mean sin has no effect on us, it will be a battle we will have to fight until we either die or are taken up to heaven. But we can also see here that we are dead to sin and alive to God. We are crucified with Christ and He lives in us. We don't have to let sin have control over us. We have choices in this battle as you can see from the bolded verbs in the verses above. The choices we make when we are faced with sinful choices and temptations will be ours to make. But God has not left us alone in this war but has given us a promise that He will always provide a way out for us when we are tempted (1 Corinthians 10:13).

In addition to that, as I have mentioned before, we can't do this by ourselves. We don't have the power in ourselves to fight this war and that is why God has promised to help us all along the way. Most importantly, He sent us His Holy Spirit to help us. The Holy Spirit is where we must draw our strength in order to resist sinning. He will speak to us in our hearts, in our minds, through other people and through the Word of God to equip us to fight this battle.

It should be clear by now that if we don't know the Word of God we are missing out on a great source of help. The more we read and study the Bible, the more the Holy Spirit will be able to speak to us about how to resist sin and temptation using the Word. Memorizing verses, in a way, is like getting ammunition for this battle. We can use them to confront sin with the Word of God when we are tempted to slip. And because God's Word also trains us with principles for how we are to live our lives, knowing the Word can also redirect us toward righteousness rather than sinfulness. (See Romans 8 for a wonderful description of how the Holy Spirit helps us in this battle.)

What does this look like practically and daily? It may mean choosing a gentle and quiet attitude when people irritate us. Forgiving someone when we think they do not deserve it. Impressing the importance of the gospel on our children even on the days we would rather stay in bed or not be a mother. Being consistent in our walk with Christ, even when circumstances are not ideal around us. Pressing on when we feel overwhelmed by life's circumstances. It means putting the eternal things above the temporary in this life. I'm sure you could add your own things to this list. These are some of the things I have learned about fighting this battle against my sinful nature in the power of the Holy Spirit.

Have you ever seen someone win a game and then gloat and go on about how great they were? That is a temptation we need to be aware of here as well. Be careful that you do not become overly confident in your walk with Christ, which would lead to a fall (1 Corinthians 10:12). We need to remind ourselves that it is Christ's death and life in us that gives us victory over sin, not our actions and strength. As we make choices to resist temptation and sin, to fight against our sinful nature, we will grow spiritually. It won't be an easy stroll, it will be a hard run race, a marathon with eternal rewards.

> *"Do you not know that in a race all the runners run,*
> *but only one gets the prize?*
> *Everyone who competes in the games goes*
> *into **strict training**.*
> *They do it to get a crown that will not last;*
> *but we do it to get a crown that will last forever.*

Therefore I do not run like a man running aimlessly;
I do not fight like a man beating the air.
*No, **I beat my body and make it my slave***
So that after I have preached to others,
I myself will not be disqualified for the prize."

1 Corinthians 9:24-27 (NIV, emphasis mine)

Our human actions, as sincere as possible, cannot save us from sin. Only Christ living in us can accomplish that. But we do have a choice as to who we will follow: Christ or our worldly agenda? I am conscious that we keep repeating this concept, but nothing is more important on our spiritual journey. We need to let Christ reign in us to have victory over sin (Galatians 2:20).

Run the race in such a way as to get the prize, dear Sister!

CHAPTER EIGHT

WHY IS THIS SO HARD? PART TWO: A SPIRITUAL ENEMY

Part Two: A Spiritual Enemy

"Be self-controlled and alert.
Your enemy the devil prowls around
like a roaring lion looking for someone to devour.
Resist him, standing firm in the faith,
because you know that your brothers throughout the world
are undergoing the same kind of sufferings.
And the God of all grace,
who called you to His eternal glory in Christ,
after you have suffered a little while,
will Himself restore you and make you strong,
firm and steadfast.
To Him be the power for ever and ever. Amen"

1 Peter 5:8-11 (NIV)

Aside from the sinful nature we saw in the previous chapter, we also have to cope with an invisible enemy, Satan. He has been at war against God's people since the fall of Adam and Eve. And He will try to get you off the narrow road in any way he can.

Lucifer, also known as Satan, was created by God Himself, along with all the other fallen angels who followed him in his rebellion. They were created, just like we were created, though with a different identity and power. Satan's mission since his fall is to thwart every godly plan and to blind people from being able to come to Jesus Christ or live in His power.

He will carry out this mission until the end of time when Jesus returns and claims His bride - the church - us, and our fight will be over.

A spiritual invisible enemy can only be overcome by divine help. And God has given us weapons and equipment to fight this fight. He's given us His own presence and power through His Holy Spirit. He's given us armor to protect us in this fight along with His Word to offensively and defensively combat the enemy in the spiritual realm. And He's given us prayer to strengthen us and those in our eternal family.

> *"Finally, be strong in the Lord and in His mighty power.*
> *Put on the full armor of God so that you can take*
> *your stand against the devil's schemes.*
> *For our struggle is not against flesh and blood,*
> *but against the rulers, against the authorities,*
> *against the powers of this dark world*
> *and against the spiritual forces of evil in the heavenly realms."*

Ephesians 6:10-12 (NIV)

This is a serious fight. And to make it more complicated we are facing an unseen enemy. But look again carefully at the beginning of these verses. We are told to be strong *in the Lord*. We are to stand strong *in His mighty power*, not in our own strength and power. Since the battle is fought in the heavenly realms, and we cannot visually experience that reality, our strength needs to come from the One who rules those heavenly realms, which is God Himself. Who other than the Creator of the universe could direct us better in our struggles against those dark spiritual forces? No one, because no one else but God has that type of power and strength to help us overcome this worst and most powerful enemy.

If we have decided wholeheartedly to follow Jesus and trust Him wherever He leads us then the Holy Spirit's power is inside us and we can accomplish anything the Lord sets before us. Praise God that He did not leave us alone in this battle! We can rely on the power of the Holy Spirit in order to face and win over the enemy's tactics and temptations.

Just like in an actual human war, a soldier cannot expect to win without proper armor and preparation, so we cannot expect a good outcome if we face this enemy unprepared and unprotected. Without the armor we cannot stand. Defeat is certain.

> *"Therefore put on the full armor of God, so that when the*
> *day of evil comes, you may be able to stand your ground,*
> *and after you have done everything, to stand."*

Ephesians 6:13 (NIV)

We are told in this verse that the day of evil *will* come and we will be able to stand our ground… *'after we have done everything.'* We are told to stand after we have put on His armor. The pieces of this armor are what we need to make this stand.

> *"Stand firm then, with the belt of truth buckled*
> *around your waist,*
> *with the breastplate of righteousness in place,*
> *and with your feet fitted with the readiness*
> *that comes from the gospel of peace.*
> *In addition to all this, take up the shield of faith,*
> *with which you can extinguish all the flaming arrows of the evil one.*
> *Take the helmet of salvation*
> *and the sword of the Spirit which is the Word of God."*

Ephesians 6:14-17 (NIV)

I have pondered the meaning of these verses in the last couple of years. As I have thought and prayed through these, each piece of armor seemed to speak to me of the things I was learning. Without trying to stretch the Scriptures to fit my experiences I could see how the Lord was using these pieces of armor in my life in a way to remind me of the things He was teaching me. After seeking the Lord's help, this is my humble conclusion and understanding of what the Lord is saying to me about them, in my life situations.

On my journey, the moment I began to understand that I desperately needed a complete surgery on my heart and mind to allow God complete unrestrained access to start transforming me, I was then ready to receive truth in a fresh new way. I opened my heart and my mind to Him to transform me. This was like putting on the belt of truth for me. By definition truth means sincerity, authenticity, openness and honesty. Exactly what I wanted in my relationship with Him. The truth of God's Word and who He is, represented by the belt of truth, became a vital piece of my battle-wear. In these verses the belt of truth is the first equipment we put on because, as some scholars say, everything else is secured to it. Speaking the truth to ourselves as God reveals it to us will protect us from false teaching and keep us open to learning and hearing from God.

The second piece of armor mentioned in these verses is the breastplate of righteousness. When I acknowledged my own sin, sought His forgiveness, came to understand that His death on the cross was sufficient payment for my sins and made a willful decision to follow Him, His plans, His will for my life; I could then, figuratively, put on the breastplate of righteousness. I was now seen as righteous and God had removed my guilt and shame. Genuine, complete repentance is so crucial in order to be righteous. And that repentance must be about my own sin, the plank in my eye, and not the speck in another's eye. We cannot change anyone. Only God can do that. If we continue to hold on to sin and try to control our lives and the lives of others, we leave ourselves vulnerable to all of the enemy's attacks. God is not looking for perfect people (Luke 5:31), but for genuine repentant sinners who know they are helpless without Him. That is where our righteousness comes from.

As we think about this next piece of equipment of the armor of God it's important to think about our relationship with God and with others. Our intimacy with God is His highest priority for our lives. Without a good understanding of who God is, His character, His will for our lives, we will have no sense of direction and we will walk aimlessly (Ephesians 5:15-17). We need to become diligent, willing students of His Word, seeking the Holy Spirit's help in order to understand the meaning of the Scriptures and how to practically apply them to our lives in a way that pleases God. The shoes of the Gospel of peace, as a piece or battle armor, demonstrates to me a willingness not only to grow in my own relationship with the Lord and understand how His Gospel message works in my life daily, but also in my need and willingness to share what I have received with others and live openly for the sake of Jesus Christ. For me this means being faithful in my marriage relationship. It means standing firm when it seems like nothing is working or changing. It meant trusting God when my husband was not responsive to God's call. It means being ready to face whatever hardships come my way while remembering God is always at my side (Deuteronomy 31:8, Hebrews 13:5-6, Matthew 28:20). As I put on the shoes of the Gospel of peace I can apply the Gospel in my own life, my marriage and in my relationships with others.

The enemy will try to discourage you. He'll try to convince you that God has forgotten about you and that perhaps you should take back control of your life. The shield of faith is the weapon I need when these doubts begin to creep into my thinking. I can believe by faith that God has my best intentions in mind when He allows trials and difficulties to come my way. If I lose this perspective and start doubting God's intentions and character I become an open target for the evil one's flaming arrows. But holding up the shield of faith I can extinguish ALL these arrows. And where do we get this shield of faith? From the promises of God. Once again we see how important it is to know who we are in Christ and to know God's Word. Spend time in His Word, reading and studying it, meditating on it and applying it to your life and you will be able to use your shield of faith against the enemy. What an incredible power we have when we are clothed with His armor!

The helmet of salvation is one of the last pieces of the armor of God. In John Bunyan's classic *Pilgrim's Progress*, the main character, Christian, was certain of the truth of God's call at the beginning of his journey to follow Him. He had to walk a long and treacherous path in order to be rid of his burden and find the joy of salvation. Through this journey to the Celestial City (metaphorically heaven) he picked up pieces of armor and met friends to help him along the way. But when he came to the cross and lost his heavy burden of sin and guilt he received salvation. Wearing the helmet of salvation represents the confidence I have that I am saved once and for all and will be with Jesus in heaven when this life is over. Just as John Bunyan's Christian walked in faith, keeping his desire to make it to his destination always as his goal, so we can make it our goal to walk in faith to our heavenly goal as well. The helmet of salvation is the piece of armor I need to stop the enemy's lies. His lies that say I do not belong to God. And that when I make a mistake and sin He won't forgive me. His lies that tell me I won't make it to heaven. And that I am not really saved. I can remind myself by putting on the helmet of salvation that I am His and He will never let me go. He will continue to work on me to make me like Jesus because I have received His free gift of salvation.

God did not give us His Word as a simple book. All the words recorded in our Bibles were put there to reveal who God is and tell us His story. He chose to give us this special book so we could draw near to Him, get to know Him and His character and find strength for our journey. Since we cannot talk to God face to face, the best way to know Him and find out His purpose and plans for us is to read His Word. In this passage about armor, the Bible is called the Sword of the Spirit. A sword is a vital weapon for warfare. A necessary piece of armor for defeating the enemy. When the enemy throws lies at us or tempts us to sin, we can counterattack with the Word of God. If we do not know His Word, we can easily be defeated. And the opposite is also true. The more we know His Word, the better we can have victory over the enemy. We will be able to replace those lies with the truth of God's Word (2 Corinthians 10:5), and our minds will become less and less impenetrable by the lies and temptations of this world. As we learn to use the Word of God, our Sword will become more effective in battle and stand more firmly on the Truth.

One more thing that God shows us in this verse is the importance of prayer – prayer for our ourselves and for our fellow believers.

"And pray in the Spirit on all occasions
with all kinds of prayers and requests.
With this in mind, be alert and always keep on praying for all the saints."

Ephesians 6:18 (NIV)

The fact that this verse begins with the word *And* shows that it is attached to the rest of the passage. Prayer is also a very powerful weapon, it is direct and intimate conversation with God. To me, the phrase *pray in the Spirit* means allowing the Holy Spirit to fill me so that my prayers can be in sync with God's will. The Spirit is God's Ambassador living in us, the Helper given to us (John 14:16-17, 26) to live a life that pleases God. In communion with the Spirit, we are to pray *on all occasions* and *with all kinds of prayers and requests*. God wants to hear from us *on all occasions* - good and bad. He wants us to come to Him *With all kinds of prayers and requests*. Rejoicing in His provision, crying out to Him in trouble, expressing our trust in Him when we feel worried, asking for His strength and peace when we are fearful of the future... and more. God deeply cares about us and what we are going through in every aspect of our lives, small or big. Whether our circumstances seem possible or impossible to us, He wants us to come to Him for everything we feel, think and need.

"Come near to God and He will come near to you."

James 4:8a (NIV)

"Jesus looked at them and said,
"With man this is impossible,
but with God all things are possible.""

Matthew 19:26 (NIV)

In his book, *The Invisible War*, Chip Ingram introduces a concept I think could have a big impact on how we fight this enemy.

*"As a believer in Christ, we do not fight for victory; **we fight FROM victory**. In Christ's power, we are **invincible**. [...] That means that when we fight, we're not trying to win. We're enforcing the victory that Jesus has already secured." (emphasis mine)*

When God graciously gave us His Son to die on the cross in our place and raised Him from the dead, the biggest battle in the history of time was won on our behalf. Because of this victory death and sin no longer have victory over us (1 Corinthians 15:57). To fight *from* victory means just that - Jesus has already won the battle over sin and death. We are no longer slaves to our sinful nature, the world's temptations, and the enemy's taunting. We live our lives by the power of the Holy Spirit (Galatians 5:25) who enables us to have victory over our sins daily (Galatians 5:16). Because we fight from victory we can have victory over our wrong thoughts, motives and attitudes. We can have victory over how we feel toward our husbands and act toward them. We can have victory because we have God's promises. We can have victory because we can now see other people as God sees them. We can have victory when people hurt us, use us, manipulate us, and persecute us because Christ claimed that victory for us. We can have victory because we know that we have been crucified with Christ and our lives are now hidden in Him (Galatians 2:20).

Our lives are a succession of events, here on earth, meant to prepare us for the Day of Jesus Christ, when God will make all things new and take us to the home He has prepared for us in heaven (John 14:3). No more tears, no more sorrow, no more sickness, no more sin (Revelation 21:4). Keeping this eternal perspective is important for the health of our own marriages. A friend of mine once met Reverend Richard Wurmbrand, writer of *Tortured for Christ*. Reverend Wurmbrand said to him, "A person's suffering in marriage to obey God may be the calling He has for them, which is not totally different from a Christian suffering persecution in another country for obeying God." We know that being a Christian isn't easy, on the contrary, we are told to expect hardships (John 16:33; 1 Peter 4:12). But we also know that the victory has already been won by Jesus. So we fight ***from*** victory not ***for*** victory.

It is a wonderful truth that we are never left alone and without provision to fight this battle against the enemy. Our most powerful weapons against the evil one are God's presence and power with us through His Holy Spirit, wearing the armor of God which enables us to stand firm, and the weapons of His Word and prayer. We fight from victory because Christ has already won the battle.

"Temptation and testing (or a trial) are two sides of the same coin. Satan uses an occasion or a person to tempt us to fall; God uses the same to try us and make us stronger. This we learn in Matthew 4:1 and the book of Job."

Ruth Bell Graham in the *Women's Devotional Bible*

Not even an enemy like Satan can defeat us because *'the one that is in you is greater than the one who is in the world'* (1 John 4:4b, NIV). Claim your victory in Him and don't let the enemy lie to you about who you are and whose you are.

Leaving you with one more thought from Chip Ingram's book *The Invisible War*: *"[...] sometimes his greatest blessings are preceded by the most fierce conflict... Be on guard. Sometimes the worst of times are designed by the enemy to get you to give up on God's clear direction because he knows of the powerful and wondrous blessings that are ahead."*

Go in peace, Sister, wearing the full armor of God and stand firm!

CHAPTER NINE

PERSEVERANCE

"The Lord gets His best soldiers out of the highlands of affliction."

Charles Spurgeon

Perseverance in any trial that comes your way will grow you stronger and lead you further than anything else. Once you set your mind on God and His purposes for you in trials, you will discover power, strength and growth in faith that is incomparable. The Scriptures are rich with encouragement for this journey:

"Praise be to the God and Father of our Lord Jesus Christ!
In His great mercy He has given us new birth
into a living hope through the resurrection of Jesus Christ from the dead,
and into an inheritance that can never perish, spoil or fade -
kept in heaven for you, who through faith are shielded by God's power
until the coming of the salvation that is ready
to be revealed in the last time.
In this you greatly rejoice, though now for a little while
you may have had to suffer grief in all kinds of trials.
These have come so that your faith -
of greater worth than gold, which perishes even though refined by fire -
may be proved genuine and may result in praise,
glory and honor when Jesus Christ is revealed.
Though you have not seen Him, you love Him,
and even though you do not see Him now,
you believe in Him and are filled with an inexpressible and glorious joy,
for you are receiving the goal of your faith, the salvation of your souls."

1 Peter 1:3-9 (NIV)

In this world we will have trials. Our earthly lives are but a vapor in comparison to our eternal lives in heaven (James 4:14). In heaven we will have eternal joy. The Bible calls the length of our trials, even the hardest, a *little while.* I still struggle to fully grasp this concept because of my finite vision. When we are in the middle of hard times or seasons it certainly doesn't seem like a *little while.* But after my hard times have passed, I could see many lessons learned along the way, especially the growth and strengthening of my faith. Some difficulties may be harder than others, like the passing of a loved one or the constant state of brokenness in your marriage. But if we stay alert and look hard enough, we will find God's hand in the process of refining our souls for the great day of salvation that awaits us upon Jesus Christ's return. In addition to calling our trials and difficulties short-lived, the Bible also exhorts us to consider our trials pure joy.

"Consider it pure joy, my brothers, whenever you face trials of many kinds, because you know that the testing of your faith develops perseverance. Perseverance must finish its work so that you may be mature and complete, not lacking anything."

James 1:2-4 (NIV)

When it comes to the benefits received from facing trials, I do not want to miss out on anything the Lord has for me. These hard seasons are meant to bring us to full maturity and completeness. When you love God with all your heart, mind, strength and soul (Deuteronomy 6:5; Matthew 22:37; Luke 10:27), it becomes easier to endure trials, because you realize that *perseverance must finish its work.*

As I mentioned before, the reading of martyrs' biographies was a great source of encouragement to me. Reading about people who endured great difficulties and persecution, and grew in their faith and love for God through them, gave me increased strength to accept and face my hardships.

As you know from my story in chapter one, we have a child with Down Syndrome, born with a severe heart defect. Before he was born, there was a very strong possibility that he could remain in the hospital for many weeks or months because of his fragile state. I had to face the very reality of possibly being confined to hospital grounds for a few months or more in order to care for our little Sebastien. Of course, I understood and was more than willing to give him every fighting chance to survive, but at the same time, the reality is that I would not have been able to see the rest of my children very much for a while, not enjoy the presence of my husband and have to put my spring and summer plans on hold.

I prayed that I could represent God in a great way in this trial. I even asked Him to permit me to be a light for the people surrounding me in the hospital, staff and other parents alike. He reminded me when we try to keep our lives, we will lose them, but when we willingly offer them up for His purposes, we will find the true meaning of life (Matthew 16:25). I will not lie and tell you this was not hard at the time. It was very hard. I love my husband and children and the thought of being separated from them for an undetermined period of time brought tears to my eyes. Knowing I could have missed some precious moments brought pain to my heart. But as I poured out my heart to God, and though I still experienced a degree of sadness, I had peace knowing He would carry me through this. And He did.

I do not want to be lacking anything in my faith, and that's what I wanted to carry me through those long days. If my perseverance in this trial helped point others to Jesus, and it was all the more worth it. More than all those missed family moments, more than all those spring and summer projects, more than my precious time with my husband. The truth that God is with me and used this for His glory kept the cost and the sadness in perspective.

We serve a great God who deserves nothing but our best in every aspect of our lives. Keeping in mind that one day we will stand before Him, our tears are easier to manage, our sorrows easier to deal with knowing that He will take all those away and give us an eternal glory that far outweighs our present struggles. We will not be married anymore or be a parent, but we will live a new glorious life likely without any memory of this one. Our state of mind will be constant joy.

*"Blessed is the man who perseveres under trial,
because when he has stood the test,
he will receive the crown of life that God has
promised to those who love Him."*

James 1:12 (NIV)

We can persevere because God is always by our side, because He sent us a wonderful Helper - the Holy Spirit, and because we have the assurance that all His promises are true. When your life is in His hands and you love Him you will want to persevere in order to bring glory to Him who gave you new life and saved you from your hopeless sinful state. Our part in this is to stand firm in Christ (He will enable us to do this), trusting Him to help us persevere in this world before taking us to our heavenly home one day. As we accept the trials and hard times on this earth we can know that whatever God brings our way is for His glory and for our good. When we arrive in our heavenly home the cost of persevering through these trials will be worth it!

"Now it is God who makes both us and you stand firm in Christ. He anointed us, set His seal of ownership on us, and put His Spirit in our hearts as a deposit, guaranteeing what is to come...it is by faith you stand firm."

2 Corinthians 1:21-22, 24b (NIV)

"But there's no truer worship than to honor Him for who He is when what He is doing disappoints us. To follow Him even if everything speak against you, even if you yourself want to turn back, even if it means facing the things you fear the most."

Claudia Lehman, *Under a Silent Sky*

Bible passages on perseverance

See: Matthew 5:11-12, 38-42; Luke 6:22-23; Luke 11:5-13; 2 Corinthians 4:7-18; 2 Corinthians 6:3-10; Ephesians 3:14-21; Philippians 3:13-21; 2 Thessalonians 1:3-12; 2 Thessalonians 2:13-17; Hebrews 10:23-25, James 1:2-18; James 5:7-12; 1 Peter 3:13-15; 1 Peter 4:1-19; Jude 20-21.

What do you find the hardest about persevering? Be honest about your thoughts and your feelings and see what God does with your hurts and heartaches.

_____

_____

_____

_____

What trial are you going through right now that could use a fresh dose of faith and perseverance? Remember the words of Jesus in Matthew 7:7: *"Keep on asking, and you will receive what you ask for. Keep on seeking, and you will find. Keep on knocking, and the door will be opened to you»* (NLT)

_____

_____

_____

_____

CHAPTER TEN

A WIFE'S GODLY CHARACTER

"And man was not made for woman,
but woman was made for man."

1 Corinthians 11:9 (NLT)

Godly character is something I need to work on every day. Our society and it's ungodly culture gives us a picture and a job description of a wife that is quite different from what the Bible says. God gives us commands, promises and the truth about how we are to act toward our husbands.

As I write this we have been under restrictions with Covid-19 for over a year. And my husband has been home many months during this time. I have been tested and tried on the topic of this chapter every day since then. When you live with someone day in day out, things are bound to get hard at some point. This is because the more you get to know and spend time with someone, the more you start noticing their flaws. And the more you choose to focus on those flaws, the more that person can become an annoyance to you.

As women we can have a tendency to think we need to change our husbands. When hurt, I would think if I can keep reminding Phil how much he hurt me, surely he would realize the damage he has done, and change in order to start pleasing me. But I am not the center of the universe. In fact, my role is not to change my husband or try to make my husband change by complaining or pointing out his faults. The only person that can change someone is God. And the only One who can effectively convince my husband of these faults is the Holy Spirit.

Recently I came across a great article by Christian author Chap Bettis about the self-absorption of the wounded[1]. In a nutshell he explained that when hurt, some of us tend to become so self-absorbed in our feelings that we forget God and His teachings about how to react in those situations. Our pain becomes central in our lives and we act according to those feelings and not by the truth of God's Word.

To my shame, I have to confess that I had acted that way many times toward my husband in our first years after turning our lives over to Christ. I am not unaware of how hurtful adultery or any sin can be, but even in those circumstances we always have a choice of how we will respond. The truth of the Scriptures applied to our lives can set us free from being self-absorbed when storms hit our marriages.

God is the One who determined the order of things in life and this includes the structure of a marriage. He has set the husband as the head of marriage and family. He will be responsible before God for his family's well-being spiritually and in every other way. Husbands were created and called by God to lead us and our children. So when we complain about our husbands we are actually complaining to God since this was His design. When we challenge the way our husbands operate, we are actually challenging God. Remember that His ways are **not** our ways (Isaiah 55:8-9). And He doesn't ask us to follow or submit to our husbands only when they are worthy of being followed (1 Peter 3:1 speaking of an unbelieving husband). We are all sinners, you and I as much as our husbands. We all fall short of the glory of God (Romans 3:23) and we all stumble in many ways (James 3:2).

Our husbands were created to rule, so we must follow their leading (Genesis 3:16b). They are yearning to be accepted as leaders even though they may not be able to express it in those terms. I can guarantee that when you do not yield to the temptation to "take over," your husband will become more confident in his leadership role. We must remember, our husbands are a work in progress, just like we are (Philippians 1:6). And as wives we can destroy that God-given responsibility when we complain, nag, and start thinking we can do a better job of leading than they can. Your husband is likely to shut down under this pressure. We are actually being disobedient to God in acting this way. Just look at how Proverbs

---

[1] Chap Bettis, https://www.theapollosproject.com/emotional-blackmail-and-self-absorption/

21:9 and 27:15 expose the quarrelsome, nagging wife. Not a pretty picture! God is telling us our husbands would be more comfortable living on a corner of our roof than with us wives when we act this way. If a roof is more comfortable than our already comfortable home when I act this way, I must be really difficult to live with when I go down that path. We need not to attack one another, but grow together under the influence of the Scriptures and the Holy Spirit.

Imagine that you step out and initiate a project you know God has called and equipped you to do and instead of being supportive, your husband starts complaining about how insignificant your idea is and how this project of yours is a total waste of time. And then he actually takes over your project because, according to him, you can't possibly carry this through in the first place. How would you feel? I would most certainly feel rejected and unloved. I would probably not try again out of fear of being even more rejected than the first time.

I have acted that way towards my husband many times in our first years together and I wish I could take it all back. I need to leave Jesus in the driver's seat with my husband. That way I can sit comfortably in the passenger seat and join my husband where Jesus leads. I can guarantee, even as imperfect as our husbands are, that it is much better when we do it God's way. And the benefits of a more peaceful home, more secure children and seeing my husband grow in the Lord are *so* worth it.

Most companies have male CEOs or presidents. I believe this is because of how their brains are designed. They can focus on certain issues better than we do. I am not talking about value here but roles. Women are not inferior to men, but are equal yet created differently for different roles and purposes. That's the beauty of God's plan. If your husband told you he could give birth to a child better than you could, you would laugh - and with good reason. That's part of a woman's design. And we are designed to provide nourishment and tender care for that child as well. In the same way, leading a marriage and a family is part of God's design and purpose for the man.

Continuing this example, I love to have my husband stand by my side through the birth process, to encourage me and assure me that I can do this, and pray for me as well. Our husbands, as they lead, need our support, advice, help and encouragement that we are with them and supporting them in their role as leader.

> *"The Lord God said, "It is not good for man to be alone.*
> *I will make a helper suitable for him.""*
>
> *Genesis 2:18 (NIV)*

We must take our rightful place as a helper, and not as a substitute leader, as the Lord has designed and called us to be. Just as our husbands are the head of marriage and the family, so being a helper is our role and calling. Being a helper, which means a completer, is as important as being a leader. Remember this is not about our value and equality before God, it's about our God-designed roles and purposes. When both partners take their rightful place in the structure of marriage, things fall into place according to God's plan.

Because two sinners are coming together with baggage from their past when we marry, we will face obstacles along the way. As we both strive to love and serve each other in a godly way, God will meet us in the process. And we will both learn from our mistakes. The following quote bears repeating here as it is appropriate to meditate and is relevant to the subject of this chapter:

> *"No marriage arrives at a beautiful, stable place without pain."*
>
> Charles Price, *Gender and Sexuality series*

As God has shown me through this journey, pain and suffering can draw me closer to God. Whether or not your partner wants to work on your relationship should not determine your decision to follow the Lord by following your husband. If we are called to stand alone for a season, God is more than able to meet us there.

As you seek to be a helper to your husband you will have times of disagreement. If you humbly and graciously give your husband advice and he chooses not to listen to it, you are *not* responsible for his decision. You can give advice, but you cannot force a person to do anything. If your husband ends up going the wrong way or makes a decision that does not turn out well, never, never say, "I told you so" and then tell him he is a bad leader, how he should have listened to you, how much you are disappointed in him and so on. You are on the same team. You need to come alongside him and encourage him to try again in whatever the matter concerns.

Do you enjoy being nagged and having your failures pointed out again and again? Neither does your husband. Your focus needs to be redirected to forgiveness as Jesus told us to do. And when your husband says he is sorry, forgive him and let it go! Rehashing the past will not do good but rather only harm.

> *"I am amazed at how many individuals mess*
> *up every new day with yesterday."*

Gary Chapman

Thinking about how much Jesus has forgiven me helps me in those moments when I need to forgive my husband. When you remember where you came from and how much you have grown, it helps you remember that your husband is also a work in progress. We are only here on earth for a short time to accomplish God's purposes and callings in our marriages, families, churches, and communities. We must keep this bigger and eternal perspective in mind before reacting to our circumstances. Ask the Lord to help you respond to your husband as a fellow worker in the Kingdom.

In addition to committing to not trying to change our husbands and submitting to God's order of marriage and family, we also must encourage our husbands in their God-given roles. One of the best things we can give our husbands is our encouragement. If we stop and think about the responsibility God has given them and for which they will be responsible before God, it should make us appreciate their role. They are to lead, protect, provide, teach, train, and admonish. In essence they are family shepherds. They are responsible for us and for our children's spiritual well-being. They will have to answer to God directly for how they took care of us. I remember times when my husband shared with me how hard it was for him to carry this responsibility. I am grateful that he was able to do this as it helped me to know how to support and pray for him.

Criticising or comparing your husband's abilities with other men or ideals is damaging for your husband and for yourself. This can be done in different ways. You may announce subtly or openly what other men are doing. You could leave articles or books lying around the house to hint at where you think he is failing. You could ask other people, who don't need to know, to pray for your husband in specific areas. Or you may post Bible verses around the house to try to convict him to change his actions. Stop tearing down your home and family by focusing on things that are not your business, except to take privately to the Lord. Look for the things he is actually doing right and don't focus on everything you think he should be doing. Rather, focus on what the Lord wants to do in *you*.

How can we keep our eyes on encouraging our husbands in what they are doing and not focusing on their weaknesses? Here are a few practical examples:

- **Pray for Him**
  As he starts his day and throughout the day make this a priority. Pray for his heart and mind, that they might be open to listen and receive God's truth. *The Power of a Praying Wife* by Stormie Omartian has some good ideas to help with this.

- **Make a List of All the Things he is Doing for you and Express your Gratitude and Appreciation**
  Once you start paying attention to the things he does, you will be amazed at how much he is doing! When you stop focusing on the negative, you begin to see things in a different perspective.

  Put a note somewhere he will find it (on the breakfast table, in his lunch bag, a sticky note attached to his agenda) or text him and let him know you appreciate how hard he works for your family. At times when I listened to the Holy Spirit's promptings in this, Phil would come home and tell me it was timely as he was having a hard day.

  And yes, God did guide me to do these things during the hard seasons in our marriage as well. Sometimes I did not feel like doing it, but I was reminded that obedience to the Father is more important than my feelings. I knew that if He asked me to do something hard, He surely had a great plan down the road for it.

- **Encourage him to Find Godly Friends or a Men's Group**

  God did not create us to do life alone. Our husbands need other godly men to encourage them to grow in their walk with the Lord. We need each other as a Body of Christ to grow and to be accountable. Encourage your husband to find such men or possibly a group, but don't nag him if he is not ready. Pray for God to bring men into his life that would be able to teach him, love him, and fellowship with him.

- **Express to him How Much you Love him, are Committed to him, and are Willing to Stand by his Side no Matter What**

  Remember on your wedding day when you stood facing your husband and exchanged vows with him? No one could have convinced you on that day to think about leaving the man standing in front of you. While you might still experience those feelings or bliss from time to time, certainly you do not feel that way all the time. Like all human beings, he will make mistakes, hurt your feelings or let you down. Those are the times you need to remember the vows you made to each other on that wedding day. The vows are a lifetime commitment, and God does not take them lightly. Our commitment to each other does not depend on how we feel, but on honoring God through thick and thin. We need to honor our vows by faith if not any other way.

- **Ask him How you can Help to Lighten his Burden**

  Sometimes your husband will feel overwhelmed by the daily responsibilities he carries. Offer to help relieve some of the burden of the things he has to do. While it might not always be possible for you to follow through on what he suggests, knowing that you are willing to go the extra mile will surely encourage him.

Some days I sense God leading me in an area where my husband might need my help. God knows your husband better than you ever will, so ask Him how you can be of help. It may be as simple as listening to him after a hard day at work or greeting him at the door with a smile when he comes home.

Your marriage should be the second closest relationship you will ever have after your relationship with God. Be attentive and study your husband. Learn his needs and the things that make him happy. Then serve the Lord by serving your husband. Be creative with ideas of your own to support and encourage your husband, and watch what God does with it.

- **Plan a Date Night**

  It is important to keep your relationship alive. This is especially true if you have children. See how this works out for your schedule. But don't just talk about it, plan it and make it happen.

"Only with time do we really learn who the other person is and come to love the person for him- or herself and not just for the feelings and experiences they give us." Timothy Keller, *The Meaning of Marriage*

God is in the business of changing people. He is the one who designed the structure of marriage and created our roles as partners. As wives we are called and equipped by the Lord to be our husbands' helpers. Encouraging and supporting our husbands as they serve and lead us and our families is a vital part of our role as wives. Trust the Lord to work in and through your husband and accept him as God's provision for your care and protection.

I have compiled a list of verses and Bible passages on marriage and how we are to love and care for our husbands. As a follow up to this chapter take the time to read these passages from this perspective. Ask our loving Father what He wants you to learn afresh from these passages, what He is convicting you to bring in repentance to Him, and then in obedience and faith do what He says. We must remember that no growth will occur if we try to get a quick fix or only skim through the rough lines. We will reap temporary results. God will only honor genuine efforts to seek His ways and that requires hard work and hard choices. May you be blessed by going through these life transforming passages. Another idea might be to journal all these down and record your thoughts and insights on what the Holy Spirit points out.

Passages that apply to wives in marriage

See: Genesis 1:27-28; Proverbs 12:4; Proverbs 14:1; Proverbs 19:14; Proverbs 21:19; Proverbs 25:24; Proverbs 27:15-16; Proverbs 31:10-31; Ecclesiastes 4:9-12; Song of Solomon 2:16; Malachi 2:13-16; Matthew 19:4-6; Mark 10:6-9; 1 Corinthians 7:10-17, 28b-31, 39-40; Ephesians 5:22-24, 33; Colossians 3:18; 1 Timothy 3:11; Titus 2:3-5; Hebrews 13:4; 1 Peter 3:1-6; 1 Peter 4:11.

What passages struck you? Why?

_____

_____

_____

_____

_____

In what areas did the Spirit open your eyes? What actions has He asked you to carry?

_____

_____

_____

_____

_____

Passages on love

See: Proverbs 3:3-4; Song of Solomon 2:16; Song of Solomon 8:6-7; John 15:12-14; Romans 12:9-12; Romans 13:8; 1 Corinthians 13:4-8, 13; Ephesians 4:2-6, 31-32; Philippians 2:1-11; Colossians 3:1-17; 1 Thessalonians 5:11; Hebrews 13:1; 1 Peter 4:8; 1 John 4:7-21; 2 John 6; 3 John 11.

Love can be hard to demonstrate when hurt. What do you find challenging through the reading of those verses?

_____

_____

_____

_____

_____

_____

Let us be transformed inside out that we might not hinder the Good News of our Lord and Savior Jesus Christ!

CHAPTER ELEVEN

TIME WELL SPENT

"Do not store up treasures here on earth,
where moths eat them and rust destroys them,
and where thieves break in and steal.
Store your treasures in heaven,
where moths and rust cannot destroy,
and thieves do not break in and steal.
Wherever your treasure is,
there the desires of your heart will also be."

Matthew 6:19-21 (NLT, emphasis mine)

China Inland Mission founder and missionary, Hudson Taylor, echoes the words of Jesus in the book of Matthew:

"The security of Christians is too often found in their possessions,
not in their heavenly prize."

What you and I choose to focus on will determine our reactions to the circumstances of our life. Dan DeHaan, in his book *The God You Can Know,* describes this phenomena well:

*"Mind-preoccupation will determine our goals, our enjoyment of reality, and our ability to affect other people's lives for the better. In order for Christlike behavior to be a whole of life, **there must be a preoccupation with "things above."** It is the conscious worship of God's character that conforms us to what we worship. **We always become what we worship.** That is a law within even earthly relationships. What you bow down before, you become enamored with. Some people ponder and brood over their past victories and failures. They become past-conscious. Their day begins with the past. As a result, they can*

*never really be what they should be right now, for this moment. Other people are preoccupied with position, possessions or pleasures. They actually worship these things. Whether they know it or not, those are the things that control their thoughts throughout the day. They are becoming what they worship. Obviously, if we choose to worship that which is passing away, we reap the fruit of an equally unstable mind and character. **Find me a worshiper of God, and I will show you a stable man with his mind in control, ready to meet the present hour with refreshment from above.**" (emphasis mine)*

Whatever we choose to focus on will control us, dominate our thoughts, affect our daily decisions and ultimately determine the depth of our relationship with God. It can go as deep as affecting our health. If we say we want God's best for our life, then our decisions and our actions must match our words.

> *"But don't just listen to God's Word.*
> *You must do what it says.*
> *Otherwise, you are only fooling yourselves."*
>
> *James 1:22 (NLT)*

How do we attain such a lifestyle? We discussed in chapter 5 that our strength for the journey comes from time spent with God. Let's explore that more in this chapter, by looking at how we spend our time and our days.

When I started taking out of my life everything that was crowding God out, my relationship with Him began to change a great deal. Almost ten years ago, my husband made the decision to remove our cable subscription. It had and still has a profound positive impact on our marriage and on our family. God laid it on my husband's heart that all the time he was spending watching sports or other shows, was time he could be spending working on his marriage and his family instead. He realized how all that time had no eternal value or impact whatsoever. He still feels that way today, even more so than before.

Our time on this earth is very short. The Bible compares our lives to a vapor, or as some versions put it, like the morning mist (Psalm 39:4-5, Psalm 90: 12, James 4:14). And if we consider that we sleep about one third of our lives, we could then say that we only "live," or are awake, for about two thirds of our vaporous lives. That is so incredibly short. What kind of impact do we want to have? What inheritance do we want to leave for our children? What future do we want to leave for our friends and neighbors? What are we allowing to crowd out our precious time with God and for God?

In this day and age the constant surge and pressure of social media can be a consuming hindrance to our time with the Lord. Days can be filled with keeping up-to-date on other people's lives on Facebook, Twitter and Instagram to name a few. We may know everything that is going on in other people's lives, while being completely oblivious to what God has so graciously given us before our very eyes - our husband and perhaps children. What are we telling our family members when texts become such an urgency to answer, when shopping online for the latest gadget becomes our day's focus and they are ignored?

I was greatly impacted years ago by one particular message from Charles Stanley. In essence, he mentioned that if our time with God represents a quick ten minutes in the morning, an even quicker prayer before we are out the door to do what needs to be done, and then expect to live out the Christian life victoriously, we will ultimately fail. The world will win over us every single day in this case.

Over nine years ago I realized my Facebook account was more important than raising my children. I was spending more time thinking about it than thinking about God. It became my way to escape reality. It has now become an annoyance, because my focus has changed. My thoughts are consumed with God, His Word and striving to keep developing my relationship with my Savior. I claimed to be a Christian yet my life, to my husband and my children, was a weak representation of His Son. I attended church every Sunday, Bible study twice a month, but my day-to-day life was still enslaved by the world's temptations and interests. I wasn't walking victoriously because God did not have first place in my life. The quality of time I gave Him was certainly not an image of what my words were saying on Sunday morning or during my Bible study. This is what Jesus meant when He spoke those words, quoted from the book of Isaiah:

> *"These people honor me with their lips, but*
> *their hearts are far away from me."*
>
> *Matthew 15:8 (NLT)*

My husband and I have eight children, so an actual "quiet" time during the day is nearly impossible. When we both decided to wake up an hour and a half before our children and spend time with God, our spiritual lives began changing at a quicker pace. When we read the Word of God, pray, and listen to God, we can actually hear Him speak to our hearts, because nothing else is crowding that voice out. I'm not saying this is how you should manage your own schedule. You'll need to see what works for you. But realize that time with the Lord is vital for your soul, your spiritual health and the health of your family.

In the hard seasons of my marriage my quiet time was at dawn and before bed. Twice because it's what kept me going every single day. It's what kept my focus on the eternal things. It kept my eyes focused on Jesus, and not my circumstances. That's what helped me to react to my marriage circumstances with the truth of God's Word, and not my emotions.

> *"Finally, brothers, whatever is true, whatever is noble,*
> *whatever is right, whatever is pure, whatever*
> *is lovely, whatever is admirable -*
> *if anything is excellent or praiseworthy - think about such things."*
>
> *Philippians 4:8 (NIV)*

I strongly suggest you evaluate what you permit your mind to think on. This can be made evident in many different ways. Some of these things mentioned below are things other women have shared with me:

- **Dabbling in the Occult**
  Reading horoscopes, astrological signs, and having your palms or future read is not just unwise, it's like playing with fire! These are detestable practices in God's eyes. Not only is it playing with the enemy, it brings no glory to, and in fact, it dishonors God. He calls for believers to trust Him, so He can lead us where He sees best for us, not for us to team up with Satan and walk in the occult. Remember that no one can serve two masters (Matthew 6:24). Author, speaker and evangelist Angus Buchan once said *"There are no fair-weather Christians, you are either in or you are out."*

See: Leviticus 20:6-8; Deuteronomy 18:9-14; 2 Kings 21:1-11; 1 Chronicles 10:13-14; 2 Chronicles 33:1-19; Isaiah 8:19-20; Isaiah 45:18-19; Isaiah 46:8-10; Isaiah 47:10-14; Isaiah 65:1-5; Ezekiel 13:17-23; Daniel 2:1-28 (only God can interpret dreams); Acts 19:8-20; 2 Corinthians 7:1; Galatians 5:19-20; Galatians 6:7-8; Philippians 4:8; Revelation 21:8.

- **Enamored with Romance**

  Novels, movies and television programs that feed an ungodly desire for fantasy, romance and eroticism are damaging to our relationships with our husband. Even some books who claim to be Christian need to be taken with caution. Romance can be a pleasant aspect of marriage but we should not base our whole lives on it. You will be greatly deceived. Filling your minds with fantasy romance could make your heart discontented with your own husband. Just as no wife can compete with pornography, so no husband can compete with the perfect men portrayed in romance novels and movies.

  See: Proverbs 4:23; Proverbs 31:-11-12, 30; Matthew 5:27-28 (can be applied to women as well); Romans 13:13; 1 Corinthians 6:18; 1 Corinthians 10:31; Galatians 5:16; Philippians 4:8; Colossians 3:1-10; 1 Thessalonians 4:3-5; 2 Timothy 2:22; Titus 2:3-5; 1 John 2:16.

- **Trapped in Pornography**

  Recently I learned about an increase in women being trapped in the addiction of pornography. Some attribute it to the increase of social media use and partners not actively working on their marriages. Women, not having their sexual or emotional needs met, may then turn to these very explicit and unrealistic videos and images. The real danger in that is to completely lose track with the original God-intended purpose of sexuality which is for a married couple only (Hebrews 13:4). Experts say pornography has a very profound negative effect on the brain, similar to taking drugs. It isolates you, fuels shame, destroys your self-image and ruins relationships. It awakens areas of your brain that were not created for those purposes and it is then very difficult to "reprogram" these areas to think godly, mature sexual thoughts, solely focused on your husband. If you struggle in this area, please reach out *now*, as it is very difficult to find freedom from that darkness on your own (James 5:16). Reaching out to other godly mature believers will enable you to become accountable to God for these temptations which are too powerful to resist on your own. The Holy Spirit can most certainly use others to speak loving conviction over your circumstances. We need to remember that no unforgiven sexually immoral person will enter the Kingdom of Heaven. (1 Corinthians 6:9) It is a sobering but serious warning. God will always provide a way of escape when we are tempted beyond our strength (1 Corinthians 10:13) through the Holy Spirit's power.

See: Exodus 20:17; Job 31:1-12; Psalm 119:37; Proverbs 6:32-33; Matthew 5:27-29; Matthew 6:22-23; Mark 7:20-23; Romans 13:12-14; 1 Corinthians 6:9-13, 18-20; 1 Corinthians 10:12-13; Galatians 5:1, 13-26; Ephesians 4:1, 17-24, 30; Ephesians 5:1-20; Ephesians 6:10-18; Philippians 4:8; Colossians 3:1-10; 1 Thessalonians 4:1-8; 1 Thessalonians 5:22; 2 Timothy 2:22; James 1:13-15; James 4:4-10; 1 Peter 2:11-12; 2 Peter 2:19b; 1 John 1:8-10; 1 John 2:15-29; 1 John 3:4-10; Jude 5-8.

- **Acting Inappropriately around Other Men**
  Whether you are in a good or a bad season in your marriage, how you act, talk, and dress around other men (and others) should reflect God's glory and bring honor to your husband. Your behavior should in no way give out the message that you are looking for attention or displeased with your husband. It is not honorable to God and brings dishonor to His Mighty Name. I will take the opportunity here to bring your attention to how you dress and the message it conveys to other people around you, especially men. While you are not responsible for how men look or think about you, you are responsible for attracting their attention in an ungodly way by the way you dress, act or talk.

As I am certain you would not appreciate another woman trying to seduce your husband by flaunting her body in tight fitting, revealing and inappropriate clothing, so be very careful how you dress as your apparel also communicates a message to the world. Followers of Christ should be different in all aspects of their lives, including clothing, for which the main purpose is simply to cover our bodies. Fashion is not a matter Christian women need to worry about. Being modest is rather where our aim should be as daughters of the King of kings. Similarly, be watchful how you speak and act toward other men. For instance, you should never find yourself alone with another man (except a health care professional, perhaps), whether he is married or not. Your words around other men need to be appropriate, respectful, gentle, and in no way convey that you are trying to gain their attention or approval. Our approval comes from God alone and as a married woman, you belong to your husband only. No matter what marital issues you are facing, always honor your husband by all your actions. Acting inappropriately around other men is basically being a seductress. In Proverbs 2, 5, 6 and 7, you will notice that these ungodly ways lead men to spiritual death. And one day, you will have to answer to God for the ways you have tried to seduce other men, if you do not repent of this type of attitude. You and I were made in the image of God, therefore let's honor Him as best we can in all our ways.

See: Genesis 1:26-27; 1 Samuel 16:7; Proverbs 11:22; Romans 12:2; 1 Corinthians 6:19-20; 1 Corinthians 10:31; Galatians 6:7; Philippians 2:3; Colossians 3:12; 1 Timothy 2:9-10; 1 Peter 3:3-4.

- **Distracted by News and Blogs**
Reading popular magazines, tabloids or celebrity news, following blogs and trending topics can be all-consuming. By doing this we are not only filling our mind with unhealthy input, but we are wasting time that can be put to better use for building our homes. These print and other media sources can be mostly gossip and the world's ideas of how we should run our lives. Too much time spent

here will change our perspective and drown out the Bible's view of who we are in Christ and how we are to live to please Him.

See: 1 Chronicles 28:9-10; Jeremiah 17:5-10; Romans 12:1-2; Philippians 1:27; Philippians 2:12a-16a; Philippians 3:13-14; Philippians 4:8; Colossians 3:1-4; 2 Timothy 1:6-7; 2 Timothy 2:4; Hebrews 2:1-5; Hebrews 3:12-14.

- **Fixated on Body Image, Diet and Exercise**

  Being healthy and staying active is important so we can pursue God's callings for our lives. But we can become fixated on how we look. I have personally struggled with this, especially after my husband began confessing his pornography addiction. I blamed myself, saying 'if I could only look a certain way, he would not struggle with this issue.' That is a lie! We are to keep our bodies healthy, but we are not to worship them or try to impress people and win friends by how we look. Mindless eating, following the latest trendy diet, stress eating, eating beyond our needs or to reduce stress and escape reality are also ways we can fixate on our image. Food is made to give us energy so we can serve God better and have the strength to carry out our responsibilities and callings well. While treats are good once in a while or for a celebration, we need to be careful not to start worshiping food and living for the next meal. Like any other sin that does not satisfy, it will only fill the void temporarily. God's view of us goes beyond physical appearance and looks to people's hearts. Our body image does not change how He thinks of us.

  See: 1 Samuel 16:7; Psalm 139:14; Proverbs 31:30; Ecclesiastes 11:10; Mark 7:17-23; Romans 12:1-2; Romans 14:1-23; 1 Corinthians 6:19-20; 2 Corinthians 10:5; Philippians 4:8; 1 Timothy 4:8-10; 2 Timothy 3:1-9.

- **Preoccupied with Outward Appearances**

  Clothes are necessary but they can easily become more than a need. Dressing in a more attractive way to garner attention from others for the wrong reasons can be dangerous. When Phil admitted his pornography addiction this became another problem for me. By trying to please my husband and turn his mind away from other women I became preoccupied with how I looked. Peter tells us in his first letter: *"Do not be concerned about the outward beauty of fancy hairstyles, expensive jewelry, or beautiful clothes. You should clothe yourselves instead with the beauty that comes from within, the unfading beauty of a gentle and quiet spirit,* **which is so precious to God.***" (1 Peter 3:3-4, NLT, emphasis mine).* As we strive to represent Jesus well on this earth, we need to have the same priority Peter mentions here: inward beauty first, then outward. I had to ask myself what kind of attention was I wanting from the way I was dressing? And what example was I giving to my daughters by my example? Similarly, we can overly focus on the appearance of our homes, always following the latest trends and putting much energy and money into temporary, material things.

See: Proverbs 11:22; Romans 12:1-2; 1 Corinthians 6:12-20; 2 Corinthians 10:5; Philippians 4:8; 1 Timothy 2:9; 2 Timothy 3:1-9; 1 Peter 3:3-4.

• **Edged in Wrong Friendships**
Even though Jesus was a friend of sinners, there are many warnings in the Bible about choosing friends wisely, because "bad company corrupts good character" (1 Corinthians 15:33). Wrong friendships lead us astray. In his book *Surviving in an Angry World*, Dr. Charles Stanley has wise advice:

"In your home, workplace, and any other area of your personal environment, choose to distance yourself from people and activities that display these characteristics: violence, vengeance, vindictiveness, vacillation and violation." Friendship with a gossip, a quick-tempered person, a rebellious person, a self-indulgent person, a sexually immoral person, an always indecisive person will ultimately drag you down and have a very negative effect on your faith and life. While we are called to bring the Good News *to* all

the world, we are not called to be a friend *of* the world. The book *Boundaries* by Henry Cloud and John Townsend has a chapter devoted to having healthy boundaries in friendships. It is a great read if you might have issues in this area.

See: Psalm 1; Proverbs 1:10, 15; Proverbs 2:20; Proverbs 13:20; Proverbs 22:24-25; 1 Corinthians 15:33; 2 Timothy 3:1-5.

- **Using Drugs, Prescription Medication or Alcohol**
  While the occasional drinking of wine is not a sin if you do not get drunk, the daily or constant need for alcohol is a sign of an addiction infiltrating your life. On the other hand, using illegal or legal drugs (marijuana, cocaine, heroine and the likes), no matter what the world claims, is a sin. And when it comes to prescription medication, while we might need it in order to heal from an infection or disease for a certain amount of time, overuse of it is a sin. What I mean by that is using it beyond what your body needs. This could be seen in exaggerating your symptoms, not taking care of yourself properly or finding a doctor who will give you what you want. As in all aspects of our lives, we need to evaluate why we do what we do. Are our actions glorifying God? Will the use of these substances hinder our walk with Christ? What is the purpose of using these substances? Such questions can reveal much truth about our actions. As many other sins, alcohol, drugs and prescription medication are not meant to be used as a mode of escapism from our worries or life's troubles. They can greatly affect our health in very negative ways.

See: Proverbs 20:1; Proverbs 22:3; Proverbs 23:29-35; Proverbs 25:28; Isaiah 5:11; John 8:36; Romans 12:1-2; Romans 13:13-14; Romans 14:21; 1 Corinthians 3:16-17; 1 Corinthians 6:9-11, 19-20; 1 Corinthians 8:9-10; 1 Corinthians 10:13; 2 Corinthians 6:3; Galatians 5:16-21; Ephesians 5:15-20; Philippians 4:5; Philippians 4:8, 1 Thessalonians 5:6-8; 1 Timothy 3:2-3, 8; Titus 2:12; Hebrews 10:26; 1 Peter 1:13-19; 1 Peter 4:1-5; 1 Peter 5:6-11; 2 Peter 2:19-20.

- **Escaping Responsibilities with Work or Ministry**

  While work and ministry can be fulfilling, they should not be opportunities to escape our God-given roles as wives or mothers. Similarly, if we use work or ministry to fill an emotional void, we will still feel that emptiness no matter how hard we try to cover it. If we become successful in these areas, but forfeit our responsibilities as wives or mothers to care for our homes first, then again we bring dishonor to God. If you are struggling in your marriage, it is better that you leave the ministry for a while and work at making things right with your husband. Ministries and employment opportunities will always be there. While you might not be able to take a leave of absence from work, focusing on what's important and eternal will help you. If you have children, I would strongly suggest you evaluate if work is necessary. Nurturing, caring for, training and discipling your children that only you as parents can do can have an incredible eternal impact and lay a solid foundation for the rest of their lives. Evaluate if ministry and work fits your schedule and if you have ample time to serve God honorably at this season in your life without sacrificing one for the other. If you sacrifice your calling as a wife and mother for ministry and work you risk burning out emotionally and physically, and leaving your marriage and family in shambles.

  See: Proverbs 14:1; Proverbs 31:10-31; Ephesians 3:10-11; Ephesians 5:15-17; Colossians 3:23-24; Titus 2:4-5.

- **Living a Hypocritical Lifestyle**

  We should not be acting a certain way in church, or Bible study and being someone else the remainder of the time. We are called to walk the walk, not just talk the talk. Jerry Bridges addresses numerous aspects of the church living in hypocrisy in his book *Respectable Sins*. In a nutshell, if we worship God on Sunday morning, but live in envy, gossip, slander, strife, sexual immorality, bitterness, resentment and the likes, we are deceiving ourselves. We might wear masks in church and in front of believers, but God sees through it all and with time so will others. Who we are when not in public is what matters. Our kids, and others, will see right through our facade and may turn away from the faith because of our hypocrisy. It is so very important that we bring to the Lord what really bothers us in order for Him to set us free from these destructives attitudes and actions that are harming our relationships with Him and others. The Bible contains many warnings about living such a lifestyle. It even goes to say that people who live this way will not inherit the Kingdom of God. We should seriously heed these warnings as we do not know when our Savior is coming back. Jesus issues a wake-up call for all of us in Luke 18:8b: "But when the Son of Man returns, how many will He find on the earth who have faith?" How do you and I want to be found upon His return?

See: Job 8:13; Proverbs 11:13; Proverbs 20:19; Proverbs 26:22; Ecclesiastes 12:13-14; Matthew 6:1, 16-18; Matthew 7:1-6, 21-23; Matthew 15:7-9; Matthew 23:27-28; Mark 7:6; Luke 6:37-42, 46; Luke 12:2; Luke 16:10-15; Luke 20:46-47; Romans 2:1-5; Romans 10:3; Romans 13:11; Galatians 5:13-26; Galatians 6:3-5; Philippians 4:8; 2 Thessalonians 3:11-12; 2 Timothy 3:1-5; Titus 1:16; James 1:21-26; James 2:14-26; James 3:1, 1 Peter 2:16; 1 John 2:1-6; 1 John 4:20; Revelation 3:16; Revelation 21:8.

- **Denying God Access to Our Issues**
  Not giving God access to healing our damaged emotions, hurts and heartaches can leave us feeling empty, lonely, depressed, angry, exhausted and more. We all have issues and baggage that we bring into our marriage relationship. While we might not heal from all our past immediately, turning over our issues to our loving Father, will make our lives lighter and freer. We might still feel the sting of an emotional wound, but we will be assured that the One who made us is working out His purposes in our lives in His time. First Peter 5:7 tells us to "*cast all your anxieties on Him, because He cares for you.*" Philippians 4:6-7 exhorts us to a similar call and assures us that "*the peace of God, which transcends all understanding will guard your hearts and mind.*" Such peace is an indicator that God

is at work in us. Being stressed out or angry with circumstances can be a sign that we are not communing with God or giving Him total access to our lives. Growth is sure to be shortcircuitted if we keep anything from our Maker.

See: Genesis 41:51 (Joseph did not let his past define him); Deuteronomy 31:6-8; Joshua 1:9; Proverbs 4:25; Isaiah 40:31; Isaiah 41:10; Isaiah 43:18-19; Isaiah 55:6; Matthew 6:15; Matthew 19:26; Luke 1:37; Luke 9:62; John 14:27; Philippians 3:12; Philippians 4:13; 1 John 1:9.

- **Overcrowding our Schedules**
  Our lives need to be guided by the Holy Spirit, not our own agendas. Different seasons call for different priorities. And so we need to carefully analyze how we choose to spend our time. The story of Mary and Martha is a great example of being over busy with things that are not important. Martha was so focused on preparing a meal that she was missing out on the teaching and presence of the Messiah in her home. Often we may resemble Martha, always hurrying to get things done, get to the next class, attend the next meeting or conference. And all the while missing out on the precious presence of God, taking time with Him, and the evidence of Jesus working in and around us. We must really learn to be counter-cultural here by being transformed by the renewing of our minds (Romans 12:1-2). Jesus told Martha that *"There is **only ONE thing worth being concerned about**. Mary has discovered it, and it will not be taken away from her." (Luke 10:42, NLT, emphasis mine)*. The key is looking at the motives of our hearts behind the choices we make. Our lives have earthly responsibilities that we cannot neglect and serving opportunities from God. Without reliance on the Holy Spirit, we will not make wise choices about our time and live out our best for God. Learning to discern the general will of God for His church and His individual will for our lives in each season of life is crucial if we want to live out a fruitful and purposeful life that reflects the image of our glorious Savior.

See: Psalm 37:7; Proverbs 3:5-6; Proverbs 23:4; Ecclesiastes 3:1-22; Matthew 6:19-21, 33-34; Matthew 11:28-30; Matthew 16:24-26; Luke 10:38-42; Romans 12:1-2; Ephesians 5:15-17; Colossians 3:23; 2 Timothy 2:4; 1 John 2:16-17.

The closer we draw to God, the more every aspect of our lives will be transformed by Him, and the freer we will feel from the world's pull toward ungodliness.

So what would a godly wife's schedule look like? With what should we replace these unhealthy habits? Sally Michael in her book *Mothers: Disciplers of the Next Generation* has great advice that not only applies to mothers, but to all women. I have summarized in my own words her ideas and added some of mine:

1. **Be in the Word daily.** As routine becomes a habit, find a time and a place. Consistency will turn all our good intentions into a reality.
2. **Meditate, meditate, meditate ON THE WORD!** Don't just read, think and ask God for help and wisdom to understand. Often, I use a journal. It forces me to ponder and memorize what I have just read. I go back to what I have written and I can clearly see how God has carried me through seasons and has grown my faith. Everyday the Holy Spirit is wanting to help us understand what we read. It is pure gold for our souls.
3. **Memorize** verses. Our family uses *The Fighter Verses* from Truth 78[2]
4. **Pray** daily, many times and with many kinds of prayers (thankful prayers, adoration prayers, confession prayers and supplication prayers and more). Ask God to purify your thoughts, to help you keep the Word in your mind and heart, and to be able to minister to others. (See 1 Thessalonians 5:16-18)
5. **Read** books about the Bible and Christian books of depth.
6. **Seek** godly counsel and strong Christian fellowship.
7. **Listen** to the preached Word, and not only on Sundays. Today, with the internet, we have unlimited access to great sermons and teachings. But again, caution here! Just because it talks about God

---

[2] Fighter Verses, https://www.truth78.org/fighter-verses

doesn't mean that it is right. One of the reasons we need to be in the Word is that you will be able to discern false prophets and teachers from righteous ones.

8. **Attend** a Bible study, if possible.

9. If possible, **find** an older Christian woman who can come alongside you and become a prayer partner and source of godly counsel.

10. **Guard your heart!** Stop in the middle of situations, look at your heart and address the attitudes and feelings, and the sin within.

11. Make **confession** a part of your daily routine. Keep short accounts with God. Every day our hearts lead us astray. We have attitudes that must be checked, desires that need to be reigned in, and actions that need to be changed because they do not honor God. We must constantly examine our hearts, discover the roots of our emotions, confess any exposed sin, and pray for God's help.

12. **Wean yourself from the world**. What we expose ourselves to will either nurture our souls or damage our souls. We need to make the best choices for how to spend our time. What influences will we allow in our lives, and which appetites will we feed?

13. If your husband is willing, make time every day to **pray with him** about your marriage, your family and that God would help unfold the work He has for the two of you together.

> *"But if you look carefully*
> *into the perfect law that sets you free,*
> *and if you do what it says*
> *and don't forget what you heard,*
> *then God will bless you for doing it."*

James 1:25 (NLT)

On page 21 of his book *The God You Can Know*, Dan DeHaan writes:

"The missing ingredient in the diet of the church today is <u>worship</u>. It is the cause of many anemic saints. They know what they should do but have little energy to do it. The early church was a worshiping church. Notice the energy they had in Acts 1 to 6."

He later adds:

> *"The early Christians took for granted that*
> *holiness was expected among believers."*

Not perfection, but holiness - being made into the image of Christ daily. Maturing. Growing. Not being stuck in the same rut of indifference and stagnation. Jesus wants access to every single area of our lives in order to transform us from the inside out. He wants His bride to be vibrant, not lacking anything. He wants His bride to be prepared to meet Him. He wants to say to us:

> *"Well done, good and faithful servant, you have been*
> *faithful with a few things; I will put you in charge of many*
> *things. Come and share your master's happiness!"*

> *Matthew 25:23 (NIV)*

The parable of the ten virgins is a passage to look at and think about how we want Him to find us when He comes back. Will we fill our lamps with oil or not? Even in the midst of a hard season in our marriages, we can welcome Him and devote our lives to following Him, for better or for worse, wherever He leads us. The risk is more than worth it! You will find abundant life like never before.

To conclude, here is great advice by world-renowned evangelist Nicky Cruz, from his book *Soul Obsession*:

"Are you waiting for a covenant from God, on a vision, on a purpose for your future? Are you longing to do great things for God - to serve Him and love Him until your dying breath? Are you wanting God to define a glorious future for you? Then stop trying to do it on your own. Don't try to set a course for your life and then ask God to bless it. Instead spend your time getting to know Him. Learn to bask in His Presence. To worship Him with abandon. To praise Him and love Him from the depths of your soul. To obey Him, even in the smallest detail. To pray and meditate on His Word. To appreciate the glory of creation. Learn to set your heart on God, and God alone, and He will take notice. There is one truth you can know for certain: God has a covenant prepared just for

you. A special plan and purpose set aside for your future. And it is more glorious than you could ever imagine on your own. If He hasn't laid this covenant on your heart, it is only because He knows you are not ready. He's waiting on you. Watching. Longing to share this vision with you and help you embrace it. And the saddest part is that many live and die having never received nor accepted this glorious future that God had in store for them."

CHAPTER TWELVE

LOVE IS THE GREATEST

"So now I am giving you a new commandment:
Love each other. Just as I have loved you,
you should love each other.
Your love for one another will prove to the world that you are my disciples."

John 13:34-35 (NLT)

If we look up the Oxford Dictionary's definition of the word *love*, we find two that are applicable to our chapter and to marriage:

1. *A feeling or disposition of deep affection or fondness for someone, typically arising from a recognition of attractive qualities, from natural affinity, or from sympathy and manifesting itself in concern for the other's welfare and pleasure in his or her presence (distinguished from sexual love); great liking, strong emotional attachment; (similarly) a feeling or disposition of benevolent attachment experienced towards a group or category of people, and (by extension) towards one's country or another impersonal object of affection.*

2. *In religious use: the benevolence and affection of God towards an individual or towards creation; (also) the affectionate devotion due to God from an individual; regard and consideration of one human being towards another prompted by a sense of a common relationship to God.*

If we look at the first definition above, we will notice it says love is *a feeling or disposition of deep affection.* Profound and deep are synonyms. It carries the idea of a large distance between a surface and it's end. These two words can be expressed in many of the following ways:

- Runs deep (*deep*)
- Experienced very strongly (*profound*)
- Very great (*profound*)
- Showing great understanding (*profound*)
- Extending far down (*deep*)

We also find the word *fondness,* which means *a feeling of love or liking for somebody, especially somebody you have known for a long time.* Fondness carries many senses: affection, love, liking, warmth, tenderness, kindness, devotion, care, endearment, feeling, sentiment, attachment, closeness, friendliness. And if we take the time to look at all of those definitions individually, it is incredibly packed with *deep* meaning and significance.

Isn't that exactly what the Bible teaches on the subject of love? I have included a list of passages on the topic of love at the end of this chapter for your reference. To grow in a deeper knowledge of what the Word of God teaches of this subject, I suggest, with the help of the Holy Spirit, that you dig deeper into it and ask for understanding as to how you can love in this way. In other words, how we can love like Jesus.

The Word of God also gives us a clear definition of love in 1 Corinthians, chapter 13. This precious chapter comes right between two chapters on spiritual gifts. We are called to love one another as Christ loves us and gave Himself up for us, in all areas of our lives:

"[...] and walk in the way of love, just as Christ loved us and gave Himself up for us as a fragrant offering and sacrifice to God." Ephesians 5:2 (NIV)

So whether you are serving the Lord at home in your marriage, in your family or through a ministry, love is to be expressed and felt through both our words and actions.

*"But now let me show you **a way of life that is best for all**. If I could speak all the languages of earth and angels, <u>but didn't love others, I would be a noisy gong or a clanging cymbal.</u> If I had the gift of prophecy, and if I understood all of God's secret plans and possessed all knowledge, and if I had such faith that I could move mountains, <u>but didn't love others, I would be nothing.</u> Love is <u>patient</u> and <u>kind</u>. Love is **not** <u>jealous</u> or <u>boastful</u> or <u>proud</u> or <u>rude</u>. It <u>does</u>*

not demand its own way. It is not irritable, and it keeps no record of being wronged. It does not rejoice about injustice but rejoices whenever the truth wins out. Love never gives up, never loses faith, is always hopeful and endures through every circumstance. (1 Corinthians 13:1-7, NLT, emphasis mine)

Now let's examine those underlined words and try to understand how the Lord expects us to love one another, how this could apply more specifically to marriage and how we can practically extend it towards our husbands.

"But didn't love others, I would be a noisy gong or a clanging cymbal"

Trying to make music or create a melody with only a gong or a cymbal would be challenging. Taken individually, these instruments would probably gather no audience. No instrumentalist could make a successful career playing them solo.

Similarly, a wife who tries to serve and care for her husband without a genuine, loving attitude and speech is *"as annoying as constant dripping on a rainy day" (Proverbs 27:15, NLT).* She merely goes through the motions without any attachment or sympathy. Let us be careful not to fall into this pattern over time and become complacent in our marriage. Complacency and indifference could lead us to resent our roles and go down the slippery slope of nagging, complaining and ultimately tearing down our home, our husband and our children.

"But didn't love others, I would be nothing"

The Word of God says that without love for others, we are nothing. We could possess all the knowledge in the world and have incredible faith, but without love, we are nothing. That's pretty clear, simple and straight to the point. The Oxford Dictionary defines *nothing* as: *something of no importance, of no concern, having no prospect of progress, of no value.*

Surely when it comes to God's Kingdom, none of us wants to fall into that category. That is why the Bible contains many warnings about watching our spiritual walk carefully. One example is Philippians 2:12:

"Dear friends, you always followed my instructions when I was with you. And now that I am away, it is even more important. Work hard to show the results of your salvation, obeying God with deep reverence and fear."

It will be much harder to be unloving if you have a deep reverence and godly fear of the Lord. Just like early in my story, when I first began my walk, I was doing all I could to serve my husband, and keep my home. But in my heart I carried no love for Christ. I had Bible head knowledge, was going to Bible study and attended church on Sundays, but my heart was full of anger and pride, which led me down a destructive road. Only when I pleaded with the Lord to show me what was wrong and completely opened my whole heart to Him, was He able to start ministering to my soul and uproot damaging attitudes from my life. Then and only then did the Bible actually become alive and transformation could take place. We need to obey the still small voice of the Holy Spirit when He confronts us gently about our sins.

"But didn't love others, I would have gained nothing"

Not only would we be of no importance without love but there is nothing to be eternally gained without love. We could be a self-sacrificing person, giving much time and effort to the poor and needy, or to a church ministry, but without love, we have gained nothing in our spiritual walk. Many people give to worthy causes, but are completely void of love for the cause itself. Perhaps, it makes them feel good or permits them to receive certain privileges, prestige and recognition, but without a genuine love for our Savior, fruitfulness will only remain minimal.

In our marriages, we could make all the necessary efforts to keep our homes clean and orderly, make sure no one lacks anything, do all our necessary chores and errands and look really good to the outside world, even to our church family, and yet be completely void of love and merely going through the motions without an actual, rich, and honest relationship with our Maker. Actions are simply actions and will never have maximal impact until we surrender to Jesus every single aspect of our lives.

"Love is patient"

As we are called to be good students of the Word of God, we will keep digging into and utilizing the Oxford Dictionary to get a deeper, more profound understanding of everything love means.

So what is the definition of patience? *Patience is (with somebody/something) the ability to <u>stay calm</u> and <u>accept a delay</u> or something annoying <u>without complaining</u>.*

As hard and difficult seasons present themselves in our marriages, as our husbands possibly commit hurtful actions or sins that affect us, we are to accept the delay of healing and restoration calmly without complaining. As our Heavenly Father is patient with us, not wanting anyone to perish in their sin (2 Peter 3:9), so are we to work at developing this kind of patience in all areas of our lives, starting in our own marriage. Notice the definition also states that we are to *calmly accept an annoying situation or person*. Jesus taught us it was easy for anyone, unbeliever or believer, to love a person who loves us (Luke 6:32). But loving when someone hurts us, betrays us, ridicules us, or persecutes us, that takes loving patience. Only through the power of the Holy Spirit can we ever display such patience. So we need to make sure we feed the Spirit and not the flesh or our selfish desires.

"And we pray this in order that you may live a life worthy of the Lord and may please Him in every way: bearing fruit in every good work, growing in the knowledge of God, being strengthened with all power according to His glorious might so that you may have great endurance and patience, and joyfully giving thanks to the Father, who has qualified you to share in the inheritance of the saints in the kingdom of light." (Colossians 1:10-12, NIV)

See also Psalm 37:7a; Proverbs 14:29; Proverbs 15:18; Proverbs 16:32; Proverbs 19:11; Romans 12:12; Galatians 5:22-23; Ephesians 4:2; Colossians 3:13; 1 Thessalonians 5:14; 2 Peter 3:9; James 5:7-8.

"Love is kind"

Kindness is the quality of being gentle, caring, and helpful. Even when the other person is not responsive to those actions. We need to guard our hearts above all else (Proverbs 4:23), lest we let anger or any other damaging attitude seep deep into our lives. We are called to repay evil with good (Romans 12:21).

When our husbands willfully or unwillingly hurt us, we are not to retaliate, but turn the other cheek (Matthew 5:38-40), go the extra mile, and keep offering ourselves as the helper God intended us to be to our husbands. We are not responsible for their actions, but we are responsible for how we answer to their actions, good or bad.

"Therefore, as God's chosen people, holy and dearly loved, clothe yourselves with compassion, kindness, humility, gentleness and patience. Bear with each other and forgive whatever grievances you may have against one another. Forgive as the Lord forgave you. And over all these virtues put on love, which binds them all together in perfect unity." (Colossians 3: 12-14, NIV)

See also Psalm 34:8; Proverbs 11:16-17; Proverbs 12:25; Proverbs 20:22; Proverbs 21:21; Proverbs 22:11; Jeremiah 9:24; Luke 6:31; Galatians 5:22-23; 1 Thessalonians 5:15; Titus 3:1-2; 2 Peter 1:5-8; 1 John 3:18; 1 John 4:12.

"Love is not jealous"

Since 1 Corinthians 13 is located between two chapters on spiritual gifts, it is logical to imply that Paul was referring to jealousy as someone who is unhappy, maybe angry and/or wishing someone else's qualities, talents or advantages. While this has no place in the church, I am equally hoping no wife is jealous towards her own husband's qualities or any other talent God might have chosen to give him. I do hope that each of us, in the body of Christ, jealousy guards the purity of marriage, and makes every effort possible to represent Christ well in this area.

Regarding our present chapter, it would be inappropriate for us as wives to compare our husbands to other husbands. Even more so to make blunt or hurtful remarks about what other men are doing in their own homes. It would also be inappropriate to become envious of other married couples and their relationships. We could quickly become discontent and angry, leaving us ungrateful for the work God could be doing in the lives of our husbands. While we can learn much from older, godly, mature couples, we should closely watch the state of our hearts in order to learn from others and not be lashing back hurtfully at our husbands for all we think they might be doing wrong. Rather we are called to be content with what the Lord chooses and allows us to experience through life, exemplifying what God commanded us in Exodus 20:17:

"You must not covet your neighbor's house. You must not covet your neighbor's wife (or husband), male or female servant, ox or donkey, or anything else that belongs to your neighbor." (addition mine, for purpose of our paragraph)

Commit to be faithful where God has placed you, looking to your own walk and your own marriage, comparing ourselves only to the standards of the Word of God.

See: Psalm 23:1; Proverbs 4:23; Proverbs 14:30; Proverbs 23:17-18; Ecclesiastes 4:4; Song of Solomon 8:6; Mark 7:20-23, Romans 12:1-21; Romans 13:8-14, 1 Corinthians 3:1-3; 2 Corinthians 10:1-6, 12, Galatians 5:16-26; Galatians 6:4-5; Philippians 2:1-4, 12-16a; 2 Timothy 2:19; Titus 3:3-8; 1 Peter 2:1-2; James 3:13-4:3.

"Love is not boastful, it is not proud"

The Oxford English Dictionary defines boastful as: *(disapproving) talking about yourself in a very proud way.*

Just like I shared with you in chapter 3, I too became very boastful in my early walk as a Christian. Even though my faith was not very serious at the time, it was not an excuse to have this type of behavior toward my husband. Maybe you too came to Christ before your husband, I urge you not to go down the same road I did. We need to stand faithfully as helpers to our husbands, with the belt of truth buckled around our waist, always wearing the breastplate of righteousness, brandishing the shield of faith with the hope that God is the One and Only who can change a person's heart. When creeping, ugly, negative thoughts come to mind, let us quickly hold up the Sword of the Spirit and bring every thought captive to the obedience of Christ (2 Corinthians 10:5). We must ask God's help in order to watch over the words of our mouths and the meditation of our hearts (Psalm 19:14, Psalm 141:3).

Satan was cast out of heaven as the result of his pride, thinking he could come to equality with God. As wives, we need to watch over our hearts and understand our rightful position before God as helpers to our husbands. Let us not think one moment we can take over their role and do it better than them.

We need to develop the same attitude that Jesus Christ had. He did not count equality with God as something to be grasped, but emptied Himself for our sake, to bring glory to God (Philippians 2:5-11). Dying to ourselves is the only way to find true fulfillment in life, to experience this abundant life Jesus promises us.

See: Psalm 10:4; Psalm 75:4-5; Proverbs 8:13; Proverbs 11:2; Proverbs 13:10; Proverbs 16:5, 18-19; Proverbs 18:12; Proverbs 21:4, 24; Proverbs 26:12; Proverbs 27:2; Proverbs 29:23; Isaiah 2:12; Jeremiah 9:23-24; Romans 3:26-28; Romans 12:1-21; 1 Corinthians 1:31-2:1; 2 Corinthians 11:30; Galatians 6:4-5; Ephesians 2:8-9; Philippians 2:1-4; 2 Timothy 3:1-5; James 4:6, 10, 16-17.

"Love is not rude, it is not irritable"

Having or showing a lack of respect for other people and their feelings, getting annoyed easily, and showing your anger is essentially what being rude and irritable means, according to the Oxford Dictionary.

Just like we have discussed more in detail in chapter 10, rudeness has no room in your life if you seek to be a godly wife. As helpers to our husbands, we need to be encouraging, not continually displaying a lack of self-control in our emotions.

As Ephesians 5:33b exhorts us *"and the wife **must** respect her husband" (emphasis mine).* Being respectful leaves no place for rudeness or irritability. When we act this way, it reveals what is really lurking beneath the surface and rooted in our hearts. Our desires must match God's heart, in all we do, otherwise our prayers and our spiritual walk will be hindered (Matthew 5:23-24, Mark 11:25-26, Ephesians 4:26). Let us learn the ways of our Savior, and leave all our irritations and anger at the foot of the Cross, where Jesus paid for them. Anger is dangerous and Jesus tells us in Matthew 5:21-24 that an angry attitude can lead us down the road to hell, facing God's judgment and wrath. So we need to be certain we are led by the Spirit and not our sinful nature. Be right with God, confess and repent of these damaging practices in your marriage, because love covers a multitude of sins (1 Peter 4:8).

See: Leviticus 19:18; 1 Chronicles 16:11; Proverbs 14:29; Proverbs 15:1; Proverbs 16:32; Proverbs 21:19, 23; Proverbs 29:11; Isaiah 59:1-2; Matthew 5:22-24; Matthew 7:12; Luke 6:31; John 13:34; John 15:12; Romans 12:1-21; 1 Corinthians 13:6; Galatians 5:16-26; Ephesians 4:29-32; Colossians 1:21-23; Colossians 3:1-18; Titus 3:2; James 1:20; James 3:6; 1 Peter 2:1-25; 1 John 3:18.

"Love does not demand its own way"

"Do nothing out of selfish ambition or vain conceit. Rather, in humility, consider others above yourselves." (Philippians 2:3, NIV). Selfishness is the complete opposite of being humble, of dying to yourself. It is contrary to the character of Jesus Christ. Therefore, as His followers, it has no room in our lives.

This could be seen in marriage as having no compassion for your husband's feelings or needs. Thinking only of yourself will lead to decisions that revolve around making you happy and comfortable, perhaps even purposefully neglecting your husband. It is closely related to anger, rudeness and irritability, and surely this type of attitude displays no love. Run away from such attitudes when they begin to surface, lest you get trapped by them and fall into the hands of the devil.

See: Psalm 119:36; Isaiah 5:20; Luke 9:23; Acts 20:24, 35; Romans 2:8; Romans 15:1-3, 1 Corinthians 10:24; 2 Corinthians 5:15; Galatians 5:24; Galatians 6:2; Ephesians 5:21; Philippians 2:21; 2 Timothy 2:4; Hebrews 13:16; James 3:16; James 4:1-2; 1 John 2:15-16; 1 John 3:17.

"Love keeps no record of being wronged"

While it might not be possible to forget all our grievances and the ones others inflicted upon us, we are called to forgive seven times seventy, which means without limit (Matthew 18:21-22).

Keeping a record of hurts only builds our own bitterness and resentment toward our husbands. Adding those damaging attitudes to your situation can only serve to add oil to an already burning fire. It could lead to you wanting revenge and retaliating against your own husband. This is not the way to find healing in your marriage, rather only more hurt. If you struggle with keeping a record of wrongs and unforgiveness, I strongly suggest you spend much time unloading your heart to Jesus as only He can free you of this dangerous attitude with His love for you.

Consider these four following passages:

"As far is the east from the west, so has He removed our transgressions from us." (Psalm 103:12, NIV)

"'Come let us settle the matter', says the Lord, "Though your sins are like scarlet, they shall be as white as snow, though they are red as crimson, they shall be like wool.'" (Isaiah 1:18, NIV)

"Therefore there is no condemnation for those who are in Christ Jesus." (Romans 8:1, NIV)

"And by that will, we have been made holy through the sacrifice of the body of Christ." (Hebrews 10:10, NIV)

If your husband is an unbeliever, consider displaying the following attitude, which we already mentioned previously:

"Wives, in the same way, submit yourselves to your own husbands so that, if any of them do not believe the word, they may be won over without words by the behavior of their wives." (1 Peter 3:1, NIV)

God will not honor destructive attitudes (Galatians 6:7), so rid yourselves of these and fall into the arms of your Savior, either for the first time or anew. Then watch what He does with your hurts both in your life and for His Kingdom.

See: Genesis 50:17; Leviticus 19:17-18; 1 Chronicles 16:11; Job 36:13; Psalm 37:8; Psalm 71:20-24; Proverbs 10:12; Proverbs 15:18; Proverbs 19:11; Proverbs 27:3; Proverbs 31:10-31; Ecclesiastes 7:9; Matthew 5:7; Matthew 6:14-15; Mark 11:25; Luke 6:37; Romans 3:10, 23; Romans 8:28-29; Romans 12:1-2, 19; Romans 15:13; 1 Corinthians 14:20; Galatians 5:19-21; Ephesians 4:22-27, 31-32; Colossians 3:8-12; 2 Timothy 2:24; Hebrews 4:16; Hebrews 12:15; James 1:19-20; James 3:14-15; 1 Peter 2:1, 23.

"Love does not rejoice about injustice"

The Oxford Dictionary defines injustice as *a lack of fairness or justice, or an unjust act or occurrence.* I went further and looked at the definition of unjust: *not based on or behaving according to what is morally right and fair.* We could summarize it by behaving in a way contrary to the Gospel.

Some of the synonyms of this word provided by the Oxford Dictionary are: discrimination, intolerance, wrong, injury, offense, evil, unjust act, villainy, sin, iniquity, misdeed, outrage, atrocity, scandal, disgrace, monstrosity, affront, grievance.

No wife striving to develop godly character should display even a hint of injustice, especially toward her husband. That would not represent submission out of reverence for Christ (Ephesians 5:21-24). The Lord is a just and loving God, and He cannot answer our prayers and help us mature if we keep anything out of His grasp. Our walk will greatly be hindered, even cut short if we dare begin walking this road.

Be watchful of your heart (Proverbs 4:23) and take time to remove all that needs removing. Resist the devil (James 4:7) or the paws of the roaring lion (1 Peter 5:8). Pray that you will remain strong, holding firmly to the hope set before you (Hebrews 6:15-18).

See: Exodus 23:1-3, 7; Leviticus 19:15; Psalm 43:1; Psalm 106:3; Proverbs 3:7-8; Proverbs 14:31; Proverbs 17:15; Proverbs 20:10; Proverbs 22:8; Proverbs 29:27; Ecclesiastes 3:16-17; Isaiah 1:17; Jeremiah 22:3-5; Lamentations 3:34-36; Micah 6:8; Zephaniah 3:5; Luke 16:10, 15; Luke 18:1-8; Romans 9:14; Romans 12:1-2; Galatians 6:7; 1 Thessalonians 4:6.

"Love rejoices when the truth wins out"

Any effort, progress, confession or repentance on your husband's part should be cause for an amazing celebration! The devil has lost his foothold in one or more areas and you are both winners as your marriage is on the road to improvement.

One temptation I had to struggle with was that I would look at all the things Phil was doing wrong as a whole, and greatly miss the little changes God had begun making in his life. Therefore, I couldn't be grateful. Once God opened my eyes to my wrong attitude, I began seeing clearly that God had already begun working in Phil's life and mine and I could give thanks.

Rejoice in every small victory! No matter how much work still needs to be done, take time to celebrate those steps forward with your husband. Let him know how you have noticed him changing, encourage him and keep praying. God is on the move and only in His time will He complete His work in you both.

"Rejoice always, pray continually, give thanks in all circumstances; for this is God's will for you in Christ Jesus." (1 Thessalonians 5:16-18, NIV)

See: Exodus 15:2; Exodus 33:14; 1 Chronicles 16:11; Psalm 16:11; Psalm 27:1; Psalm 34; Psalm 94:19; Psalm 118:1; Psalm 118:24; Psalm 145:18-19; Ecclesiastes 7:14; Isaiah 41:10; Nehemiah 8:10; Romans 15:13; Philippians 4:4; Colossians 3:17; 2 Thessalonians 3:16.

"Love never gives up and endures through every circumstance"

This part of the passage applies to the *"for better or for worse, till death do us part"* of our marriage vows. If you have ever doubted the seriousness of vows, you could read Jephthah's story in chapter 11 of the book of Judges. When we make vows to Him, He expects us to carry them faithfully, no matter how difficult it may be. You need to soberly count the cost of not fulfilling your vow and the consequences that will come as a result. No matter what the convincing argument you might have there will be consequences for disobeying God. Some come quicker than others.

He assures us in 2 Corinthians 12:9 that *"'My grace is all you need. My power works best in weakness'. So now I am glad to boast about my weaknesses, so that the power of Christ may work through me." (NLT)*

Through my hard seasons, just knowing Christ was by my side was the greatest encouragement I could have ever received.

I want to share with you this story that impacted me that fits with this passage. My father passed away 8 years ago, and as you know from my testimony, he and my mother had divorced. At the end of his life, he came to live with us multiple times after lung removal surgery and cancer treatments. One thing that kept coming back as he neared the end was his deep regret of having gone through divorce and remarriage. He wished he could have gone back, erased his immoral choices and made things right with my mother. But it was too late for him. He and his second wife had a very tense and damaging relationship, carrying much baggage from their first marriages and their past.

Satan will always tell you that the grass looks greener on the other side of the fence. But that is a lie! 1 Corinthians, chapter 7, verses 10 and 11 clearly instruct us that *"To the married I give this command (not I (Paul), but the Lord): A wife must not separate from her husband. But if she does, she must remain unmarried or else be reconciled to her husband. And a husband must not divorce his wife."*

See: Psalm 33:18; Proverbs 3:3-4; Proverbs 5:15-23 (read it from a wife's perspective); Proverbs 13:10; Isaiah 41:10; Isaiah 43:2; Matthew 19:4-6, 8; Matthew 28:20; Mark 10:9, 12; Romans 7:2-3; 1 Corinthians 7:10-11, 39; 2 Corinthians 4:16-18; 2 Corinthians 10:3-5; Colossians 3:14; Hebrews 13:4; James 4:17; 1 Peter 4:8; 2 Peter 1:10.

"Love never loses faith and is always hopeful"

Where would you and I be without hope and faith? Let us consider the following verses:

"And my righteous ones will live by faith. But I will take no pleasure in anyone who turns away." (Hebrews 10:38, NLT)

"But blessed are those who trust in the Lord and have made the Lord their hope and confidence." (Jeremiah 17:7, NLT)

"I pray that from his glorious, unlimited resources He will empower you with inner strength through His Spirit. Then Christ will make His home in your hearts as you trust in Him. Your roots will grow down into God's love and keep you strong. And may you have the power to understand, as all God's people should, how wide, how long, how high, and how deep His love is. May you experience the love of Christ, though it is too great to understand fully. Then you will be made complete with all the fullness of life and power that comes from God. Now all glory to God, who is able, through His mighty power at work within us, to accomplish infinitely more than we might ask or think. Glory to Him in the church and in Christ Jesus through all generations forever and ever! Amen." (Ephesians 3:16-21, NLT)

What a beautiful way to finish this chapter! His Word says it all in these precious verses.

Here are some extra passages for your benefit:

Psalm 31:24; Psalm 39:7; Psalm 46:10; Psalm 62:5; Psalm 71:5; Psalm 119:114; Psalm 130:5; Psalm 147:11; Proverbs 3:5-6; Proverbs 10:28; Isaiah 40:31; Micah 7:7; Matthew 17:20; Matthew 21:21-22; Mark 9:23; Mark 11:22-24; Romans 5:2; Romans 8:23-29; Romans 12:12; Romans 15:13; 1 Corinthians 15:19; 2 Corinthians 5:6-10, 14-15; Galatians 5:5; Philippians 4:13; 1 Timothy 1:19; Hebrews 10:23; Hebrews 11:1, 6.

As we learn to walk in love toward our husbands and others in our lives, let us walk faithfully and always remain hopeful that He will carry out His promises in His time and in His ways! Let us love with abandon like our sweet Savior. This way you cannot lose.

CHAPTER THIRTEEN

REPENTANCE AND FORGIVENESS

*"The world is perishing for lack of knowledge of God
and the church is famishing for want of His presence.
The instant cure of most of the religious ills
would be to enter the Presence in spiritual experience,
to become suddenly aware that we are in God
and God is in us.
This would lift us out of our pitiful narrowness
and cause our hearts to be enlarged.
This would burn away all the impurities from our lives
as the bugs and fungi were burned away by the fire that dwelt in the bush."*

A.W. Tozer

Too often we mistake confession for repentance and vice versa. They are both important, but very different. Confession is an ongoing process in our lives as we seek to keep short accounts with God of our failures and our constant need to be cleansed from the effects of our sinful nature. Confession is agreeing with God that what I did was wrong. Repentance is a lifelong decision to turn away from sin as God points out areas in our lives that need to change. It's not just a feeling, but involves a radical change of direction that results in a changed life. Let's take a closer look at both of these important disciplines in our lives and try to clear away any misconceptions we might have.

Most people know what confession is, but do not understand that in itself it does not bring salvation. Conviction is that uneasy feeling inside that comes from the Holy Spirit when you know you have done something wrong. This conviction will push you to confess your sin (agree with God that it was wrong) and ask forgiveness for your words or your actions. As believers we are called to confess our sins in order for God to cleanse us from all unrighteousness (1 John 1:9). We will need to keep practicing confession until the day we die, because even though we are forgiven for past, present and future sins, we still have to live with our sinful natures until we either die or Jesus returns. Therefore, to be able to keep growing and maturing in our faith and knowledge of God, we need to keep confessing our sins as they surface. That's what it means to keep short accounts with God.

But we can't stop there. It's not enough to just confess our sinful words or actions. We need to acknowledge and repent of the unhealthy wrong motivation that led us to speak those words or commit those actions in the first place. We must repent, or turn away, from the wrong we have done, whether in attitude, motive or action and commit to walking in obedience to Christ.

Putting this to practice regularly in our lives makes it harder for the enemy of our souls to pierce us with his arrows of doubt, guilt and temptation. It keeps our hearts clean and open for the Holy Spirit to keep ministering to us. We need to both confess and repent of our sin or we will continue to short circuit our spiritual growth greatly.

As you know from chapter one, my husband was heavily impressed by the Holy Spirit in the summer of 2020 to come to a complete repentance for the sins he committed against God and that had ultimately affected our marriage relationship. He realized that not confessing and repenting of the motives and emotions behind his actions was actually still keeping him in bondage and at greater risk of being tempted, or worse, the possibility of falling back into sexual immorality. And since most of those actions had a direct impact on me, he was not set completely free until he thoroughly confessed to me all his actions and all the motives that led him to sin in this way.

That same night, we had a very tangible visitation from the Holy Spirit. And that week, God heavily impressed on both our hearts to share all of our past - the good, the bad and the ugly. At that moment we felt more free than we ever had! It is an incredible and wonderful feeling to understand what it truly means to be set free by Christ. Fully understanding where each of us came from, helped us understand in a better way the reasons why each of us fell into the sins we committed. Some of the things Phil shared were very hurtful, but seeing my husband through the eyes of Christ is what enabled me to be able to forgive without delay and without any hint of anger. I felt joy that He was finally done believing all those lies!

Repentance is a very important part of keeping an open and honest relationship with God and others. Repentance means giving God *complete* access to all of you, by turning away from *all* your sins. It's a 180 degree change of lifestyle and thinking. Matthew 3:8 exhorts us to *"prove by the way you live that you have repented"* (NLT). In order to give God full access to our lives we must face the things in our lives that can keep us from total repentance, and accept how He has equipped us to keep our lives open to Him.

Secrets can keep you from experiencing complete repentance. Jesus came to earth, to set us free so we could have abundant life. Abundant life and spiritual freedom cannot be a reality if you are keeping secrets. You are still walking in darkness. And darkness can have no fellowship with light (Luke 11:35; 1 John 1:6). Light exposes darkness and the deeds that are done in darkness (Ephesians 5:11-14). John writes that if we think we have light but hate others, then our darkness is truly great! (1 John 2:9)

Repentance can also be hindered by our enemy. The Bible says the devil is a roaring lion seeking to devour us (1 Peter 5:8). His mission is to steal, kill and destroy (John 10:10). What are we allowing Satan to have a grip on right now by not confessing and repenting? Jesus warns us to repent or perish (See Luke 13:1-9). It is pretty clear and simple. You must turn from the enemy's evil ways and commit to walking in obedience to Christ if you wish to have abundant life and stay out of the snares of the devil.

Paul tells us in his letters that people who live this way – in their sins - will not inherit the Kingdom of God. Repentance is turning away from our sins and toward God. We can't do this on our own. We must acknowledge our great need for Him, as we cannot live victoriously without His Helper, the Holy Spirit. Jesus told His disciples that it was better for Him to leave, so that they could receive the gift of the Spirit. Imagine how this relationship is important if it is better for the Savior of the world to leave His creation so that they can receive the Helper. The Holy Spirit is God's presence and Jesus' presence living inside us simultaneously. How incredible a gift that is! Who would want to forfeit that by not confessing and repenting of their sins? Walking day to day in the presence of God, developing our relationship with our Maker is the only way to have victory over sin and hear the Holy Spirit prompting us to confess and repent. Attempts on our own terms, and with our own power, will not work in this battle against our sin and the enemy's weapons.

Jesus calls us to holy living. Matthew chapters 5 to 7 show us how His expectations are not the same as ours. His ways are not our ways (Isaiah 55:8-9). We may think that "small" sins aren't a big deal, but James compares all our sins to a spark of fire which when ignited can set a whole forest ablaze (James 3:5a). If I said to you that I have repented from my sin of adultery, but kept eyeing men on a daily basis, you would call me a hypocrite, and rightly so. Or if I would tell you that I have stopped gossiping, but still secretly call a friend or two to get juicy details about other people's lives, I would be a liar. Without repentance, our sins will continue to keep us from holy living.

Jesus warns us to count the cost of following Him, because once we put our hands to the plow, it's for life. Many people only honor Him with their lips, but their hearts are far away from Him (Matthew 15:8). If we want to follow the Lord in obedience we must make a willful commitment to keep our lives free from sin. We will undoubtedly sin to some extent because of our sinful nature. But we don't have to stay there. God has provided a way to keep our lives free from the weight of sin through regular confession and repentance, but we must be sincere in our desire to follow Him. There is no "back-up plan Sister." Jesus is plan A, plan B, plan C all the way down to plan Z and beyond! Jesus is worth the cost of our commitment.

Once we have experienced God's glorious salvation and the gift of the presence of the Holy Spirit, forgiveness becomes so much easier. In fact after pondering all our Savior did and still does for us, it should come almost naturally to forgive others who have wronged us. Jesus says:

> *"For if you forgive men when they sin against you,*
> *your Heavenly Father will also forgive you.*
> ***But if you do not** forgive men their sins,*
> *your Father will not forgive your sins."*
>
> *Matthew 6:14-15 (NIV, emphasis mine)*

Jesus' words are clear and simple. While I am not minimizing the pain of adultery, divorce or any other marital issues, our Savior has shown us the way to forgive. Notice He did not add the following:

- Only when your husband deserves it
- Only when he cleans up his act and stops sinning
- Only when he starts paying more attention to you
- Only when he actually becomes a Christian
- Only when he finally understands your 'suffering'
- Only when you can have a break from all this marital chaos
- Only if he starts acting more mature like your friend's husband

The pain of our marital issues should drive us closer to God, not further away. It should drive us to forgive quickly, so we don't become bitter and resentful. We can have a quiet time with God, go to church, and have fellowship with other Christians, but if our hearts are full of bitterness and resentment, we will not grow. And if our hearts are in that condition, we are not getting closer to God.

Our unchecked hearts will leave weeds to grow without a harvest of spiritual fruits. That's the message of the Parable of the Sower. The ground is the condition of our hearts. James writes that our faith is proven by the works we do (James 2:14-26). Our daily attitude, words and actions are reflections of what is hidden away in our hearts (Proverbs 4:23).

"You cannot serve two masters, you will either love the one and hate the other."

Jesus in Matthew 6:24 (NIV)

It's always easier to forgive when the situation doesn't directly affect us. But the Bible is crystal clear in every situation, easy or hard. If we don't forgive we will not be forgiven. No need for a theological debate or to be a Bible scholar to understand the simplicity of those words. Even a young child can understand this concept. So why then do we struggle to forgive?

Let's look at confession first. When we have done wrong, most of the time, we can feel shame, guilt and regret. It's one thing if it was a careless word spoken without thinking or we forgot to make that promised lunch for our husband. But what if it is looking lustfully at another man at the grocery store? Or hiding purchases of which we know our husband would disapprove? Then it becomes a bit harder to confess as we know full well we are in the wrong and that these actions will hurt our husbands. What if you actually committed adultery with another man? How easy would that be to confess? We know that would be very hard to do, and we also know we will greatly hurt the other person, and that trust will be deeply broken and need to be rebuilt.

Now, imagine that you are the one sinned against. We've all heard the statistics that, in general, women are much better at sharing their feelings than men. Men, on the other hand, in general, tend to be more reserved when it comes to their feelings and being open about their life and their struggles. Most of us either know that fact in writing or by experience. Knowing this, when our husbands are prompted by the Holy Spirit to confess their sins, we need to not do anything to cause them to close up and stop sharing which will cause distance to come between you. If we start yelling, calling him names or any other damaging actions I can assure you he will not want to share any other hard struggle with us for quite some time. If our husbands come to us in repentance with confession on their lips we should rejoice! They may have stopped living and believing a lie! The enemy may be losing his grip on them and our marriages are on the way to healing!

God's original plan did not include sin. And because we live in a sinful world, we will feel the emotional pain, sting, or wound of the betrayal of being sinned against. He designed us to be completely faithful in our marriages. Amidst our pain and tears, in greater measure than our damaged emotions, there should be joy. If repentance took place, God is already at work in your husband's heart, mind, and life. That is cause for a celebration! If the angels in heaven celebrate when one sinner comes to repentance, why shouldn't we? (Parable of the lost sheep, Luke 15:10)

This is why our relationship with God is so important. Without a rich relationship with God through His Holy Spirit, forgiveness will be hard to give and receive. Resentment and bitterness have a better chance of becoming our companions. As I am certain no one heads into marriage with the intention of failure, then we should make all the necessary efforts to experience this abundant, fruitful life Jesus came to give us (John

10:10b). We shouldn't scorn our husbands for making amends with God by repairing his relationship with us.

You and I need to become strong, immovable, faithful, hopeful, loving daughters of the King of kings. We can do this by basking in His holy presence, spending time in His Word, meditating on it, and asking for His help when we do not understand what to do. We have the privilege of talking to Him in prayer many times during the day. We can obey what He asks of us whether we like it or not. And we can trust Him with complete abandon.

Remember His ways are not our ways (Isaiah 55:8-9). He will most certainly not deal with our marriages and our healing journeys by our standards, our agenda, and our ways. He would not be loving if He did so. Trust Him in the good and bad. Even the deep wounds our husbands might have caused us are designed and allowed by Him to bring Him glory.

So the next time your husband comes in genuine repentance or with a hard confession to make, cry with him, give him a hug, and thank him for being so honest and transparent. Tell him you understand how hard this was to say, because it was. Remind yourselves that he can in no way go back and erase all these sins, just as you cannot go back in time either and undo yours. Encourage him that you are willing to help him, support and stand with him, and pray for and with him in his walk with Christ.

Living in the past will not change our present circumstances. Paul admonishes us in his letter to the Philippians to forget what lies behind and focus on what lies ahead. (Philippians 3:13b). Direct your attention to the healing you and your husband will experience if you place your faith and your marriage in the hands of God. And trust God for the rest while you seek to live for Him. We are not responsible for how our husbands choose to live out their lives in Christ, but we are responsible for our personal relationship with God and for the way we are being a helper to our husbands.

Keep on healing and growing and never lose hope or let go of the Father's hand. We are sojourners and pilgrims on this earth. Marriage is meant only for this side of life (Luke 20:34). One day, our tears will be wiped away and our sorrows gone! In the meantime, keep short accounts with God, give Him full access to your life, and rely on the Holy Spirit's help to confess, repent and forgive daily. The best is yet to come!

"Oh, what joy for those whose disobedience is
forgiven, whose sin is put out of sight!
Yes, what joy for those whose record
the Lord has cleared of guilt,
whose lives are lived in complete honesty!

When I refused to confess my sin, my body wasted
away, and I groaned all day long.
Day and night your hand of discipline
was heavy on me.

My strength evaporated like water in the summer heat.
Finally, I confessed all my sins to you
and stopped trying to hide my guilt.
I said to myself, "I will confess my rebellion to the Lord."

And you forgave me! All my guilt is gone.
Therefore, let all the godly pray to you
while there is still time,
that they may not drown
in the floodwaters of judgment.

For you are my hiding place; you protect me from
trouble. You surround me with songs of victory.
The Lord says, "I will guide you along the best pathway for your life.
I will advise you and watch over you.
Do not be like a senseless horse or mule that needs a
bit and bridle to keep it under control."

Many sorrows come to the wicked,
but unfailing love surrounds those who trust the Lord.
So rejoice in the Lord and be glad, all you who obey him!
Shout for joy, all you whose hearts are pure!"

Psalm 32 (NLT)

CHAPTER FOURTEEN

INTIMACY

"My lover is mine, and I am his."

Song of Songs 2:16a (NLT)

When God impressed on my heart to write about this topic, I first titled this chapter *Sexuality*. Needless to say, I felt inadequate to write about such a topic. So I turned to Christian books for guidance, hoping to find godly inspiration as to what the Lord wanted me to say about sexuality. My first attempt left me uncomfortable with most of what I read and attempted to put into my own words. I honestly think we put too much emphasis on sexuality in marriage, neglecting other very important relational issues in marriage, and found this pattern even in some Christian books. Most of the messages conveyed in those books, as I saw them, was that a healthy sexuality will lead to a great marriage. But that is not true. It takes much more than that. And in many ways this is backwards. Health in other areas of the relationship leads to healthy sexuality.

It led Phil and I to seek the Lord even more and He graciously answered our prayers. He led my husband and me to stick with our first intentions about this chapter and not to look at what others thought godly intimacy should look like or not look like. Most of these books offered tips or tricks to enhance sexuality, or make it more exciting, but we found little advice on striving to develop an overall rich and healthy relationship with the Lord as a married couple. As an exciting sexual life can be great at times, it most often is not the constant case over one's lifetime. Just as life has its ups and downs, so does our sexuality. We can experience seasons of abundance and seasons of drought, depending on what the Lord graciously allows us to go through.

As a married couple, sit down without any distractions or children around, to talk about how intimacy is reflected in your own marriage. Pray and seek the Lord's help as only He knows both of you perfectly. By seeking His standards, and through the careful reading of His Word can we approach this subject in a way that honors our Creator.

Let's not forget that our first love goes to God alone. There are no substitutes here. Anything or anyone you place before God Almighty will leave you disappointed and empty. Jesus reminds us in Matthew 22:37-38 what Deuteronomy 10:12-13 stated in the Old Testament:

> *"Jesus replied, "You must love the Lord your God with all your heart,*
> *all your soul, and all your mind.*
> *This is the first and greatest commandment.""*

Then we must also remember His words in Matthew 6:33:

> *"Seek the Kingdom of God **above all else**,*
> *and live righteously, and He will give you everything you need."*
>
> *(NLT, emphasis mine)*

Your husband might not be an adulterer or sexually immoral in other ways, but anything that comes between the two of you will ultimately affect this area of your marriage. It will not produce the close bond you so long to experience and that God wants for you. That is the reason our first love should be directed toward God. Without a rich relationship with our Maker, the rest of our lives will be lived void of the rich blessings He intends to give us when we lovingly obey His Word.

To experience *complete* oneness in the area of marital intimacy, we need to be of one mind and heart in all areas of our marriage, having no secrets or hidden agendas. Communicating clearly and regularly is paramount to understanding one another and growing in godliness as a couple. As men and women are created equal in value and love in God's image, our roles are different and so will be our approach to dealing with the issues concerning marital life.

When going through hurtful issues, opening yourself up emotionally and physically to your husband might be a very hard thing to do. I completely understand, having been there myself. But our God is a Healer and Restorer. Whether your husband repented or not, our responsibility is to be faithful to the Lord. You might not be able to open up emotionally right now, let alone offer yourself physically to him at this time, but with the Lord's help, it is possible to regain trust from hurts and pain in your marriage. Keep in mind your husband cannot undo the past. Waiting for the perfect moment of trustworthiness might leave you frustrated as well, as it will never arrive. We are all sinners and each of us needs grace both from God and extended through others.

Ask God right now where you can begin offering grace to your husband. Better small steps than none at all. God will honor your forgiving and trusting heart. Commit to do it His way, obey His leading, and leave the rest to Him. We are not called to question His judgment. Just like in my story, He asked me to buy a new wedding ring for Phil in the midst of a hard season. Remember not to lean on your own understanding (Proverbs 3:5), He often takes you on detours and unexpected turns. He loves us too much to leave us comfortable in an unhealthy place. Only when we leave our comfort zones and step out in faith to follow Him do we meet Him more personally.

Let me share with you how I still strove to honor my husband in this area, even through our very hard seasons, fully knowing he was not committed to me exclusively. We must continue to remind ourselves that in order to have abundant life, we must die to ourselves and abandon ourselves to our Savior's leading no matter where it leads us, no matter how we feel at the moment.

But before we move forward, let me repeat that if you have been the victim of domestic abuse - have been physically, emotionally, verbally abused, or mistreated sexually, these unfortunate and sad circumstances are beyond the scope of this chapter and this book. Please seek professional, godly, mature Christian counselling as you need to heal from traumatic experiences which I am not qualified to go through with you.

With time, we can all succumb to the temptation of becoming complacent with our husbands. Flaws and faults can become so annoying that we forget what first attracted us to them, routine can set us up to become too comfortable and possibly indifferent to our spouse. So a good exercise I would regularly go through is remembering how I felt toward Phil when we first met. With my parents getting a divorce when I was a young adult, it also convinced me that taking good care of my husband in all areas of marriage, to the best of my abilities, was important. I came to understand that love is a choice, not just a feeling.

Right now might be a good time to do a self check and answer a few questions. Take notes, journal them, pray about it, but most of all, seek God's advice where you could improve and bring back some of that initial commitment and zeal in your marriage.

- How did you feel towards your husband when you first started dating or courting him?
- What did you like most about him?
- What character qualities did he possess that struck you?
- How did you take care of yourself back then? How would you get ready for a date or an outing with him?
- What faults did he display that you easily overlooked?
- When did you start thinking differently about him?
- When did you stop making him a priority and have that regular time alone with him?
- When did you stop planning dates with him?
- When did your sexual life become more complacent?
- How was your communication at the beginning of your relationship?
- When he shared dreams, how would you support him? Did you share common dreams back then? If so, what happened to those?
- How did you respond when he would share difficulties or struggles?
- How was your prayer life as a couple back in those days?

There is much more to intimacy than the physical, sexual aspect of it. To experience complete oneness in this area, a couple must:
- Grow spiritually, emotionally, and mentally with one another
- Spend regular time together and enjoy each other's presence
- Have "below the surface" rich communication
- Keep each other accountable in *all* areas of your marriage
- Set boundaries as a couple
- Share each other's burdens
- Keep short accounts in regard to conflicts and settle them as soon as possible, not allowing the enemy to come between you

- Expose *all* sins, keep nothing from one another
- Commit to seeking and accomplishing the Lord's will, and serving Him wherever He leads
- Pray together, all kinds of prayers

How is this possible to attain or maintain through the hard seasons? What if your husband is an unbeliever? What if he is not repentant and keeps committing sins? Well, like we have mentioned before, you cannot force someone into something they do not want to do. You cannot change someone's mind either. But, as wives we can strive to represent God well in all the areas of our marriage mentioned above. We can prayerfully and obediently do our part and commit the results to God.

> *"Wives, in the same way submit yourselves to your own*
> *husbands so that, if any of them do not believe the word, they*
> *may be won over without words by the behavior of their wives,*
> *when they see the purity and reverence in your lives."*

1 Peter 3:1-2 (NIV)

There is power to change and live this way in a loving, obedient life committed to God. That is why our first love should go to God. Without a loving, rich, faithful relationship with our Maker, it is impossible to please Him (Hebrews 11:6). It will also be impossible for you to submit and aim to serve your husband, even more through a trial or hard season. Jesus tells us in John 15 that if we love Him we will obey Him. And He reminds us that we will have trouble in this world in John 16:33. Strive to look beyond the imperfections, fix your gaze on Jesus as you look at your husband and your marriage situation.

Here are a few things I committed to do, and would encourage you to do as well, regardless of the season in your marriage:

- **Commit Yourself Wholeheartedly to Him**
  Just like any other area of your marriage, the *for better or for worse* applies here as well. Pray with and for him in all areas of life. Make your relationship with God a priority. Honor and respect your

husband through thick and thin. Commit to carrying through *till death do us part* lovingly and faithfully.

- **Make Yourself Available**
Make time for him, possibly each day, greet him when he comes back from work, listen to him well and pay attention to his feelings and needs. Seek God as to how you can help your husband in the areas which he might be struggling.

Rely on the leading of the Holy Spirit and be sensitive to His nudgings. He knows your husband better than you ever will. What He asks you to do, He has already equipped you to do. Whether it is a difficult and emotional conversation with your husband or committing to be once again sexually available after betrayal, all things are possible with God (Luke 18:27). Do not let fear rule your heart, as the enemy would love nothing more than for your marriage to stay dysfunctional and void of intimacy and abundance (John 10:10). Remember that He who is in you is greater than he who is in the world (1 John 4:4b).

- **Make Time to be Alone with Each Other**
Phil and I experienced our greatest dates in very simple, inexpensive outings. Coffee and a donut followed by a walk in the Gatineau Hills. Driving around in a new part of our municipality and discussing what God had next for us. Be creative and have fun! If possible, make it a long weekend or a week-long vacation.

Take advantage of those moments to clear away misconceptions, deal with ongoing conflicts or hurdles. If you have children, you will feel all the more refreshed to face whatever needs to be done after those blessed breaks away from home. Time off away from daily responsibilities has a way of reviving the soul.

Spend time with God, deepen your relationship with Him and clean off your slate, enjoy His Creation, so that when you come back home, you feel like a renewed couple. Consider putting into words, a vision or a commitment the Lord impressed on your hearts. Seek His ways wholeheartedly and you will find Him every single time.

- **Keep those Moments Exclusive to your Husband**
  Don't go around sharing your most intimate conversations and sexual details with the world. If you are going through counseling and it needs to be discussed then be careful to not shame your husband.

  An important note if you have children: make every effort necessary to protect them from walking into your intimate life. Keep important conversations, disagreements and sexual details for your bedroom only. Song of Songs exhorts us many times to *"not awake love too early"* (verses 2:7, 3:5 and 8:4). Do not strip your children of their innocence too early and awaken something in them they are not ready to carry. In our home, we hug, give each other simple kisses, cuddle next to each other on the couch, but leave the rest out of our children's sight. Your children need to know you love each other as parents, not see you tear down your husband or hear intimate sexual details from the living room.

- **Seek Help to Improve your Marriage**
  There are many resources available to help couples improve their relationships. Online and in-person courses and conferences, Sunday school classes, small groups, and Bible study are all different ways to keep working on your relationship.

  If you are stuck and can't seem to get past an issue in your relationship don't isolate yourselves. You are not the only ones in this situation. Seek help through your church, support group, or counselling services. Ask the Lord to show you how you can find help during this time.

As we are on the topic of intimacy, we could not complete this chapter without discussing some aspects of sexuality. It is part of marriage and like everything else since the Fall, it is broken and often misrepresented. Here are some of the answers I found through studying God's Word:

- **Realize that Godly Marital Sexuality is a Spiritual Weapon**
  The Bible tells us in 1 Corinthians chapter 7 that: *"Do not deprive each other of sexual relations, unless you both agree to refrain from sexual intimacy for a limited time so you can give yourselves more completely to prayer. Afterwards, you should come together again so that Satan won't be able to tempt you because of your lack of self-control." (verse 5, NLT)*

  Sexuality is very powerful, which is one of the reasons the devil uses so many temptations in this area to lure people away from godly sexual intimacy. It is a means to incredible oneness in marriage as no other physical activity can create such a bond between two people. Be sensitive to your husband's needs and seek to fulfill them to the best of your ability.

- **Do not Withhold any Good Thing**
  Always be watchful of your heart (Proverbs 4:23). Do not start making excuses or play the blame game. Most men feel very close to their wives after having a sexual relationship. It is proven they are better husbands, fathers and more productive at work when sexually fulfilled. Be mindful to not deprive your husband long enough for him to find it hard to resist temptation. While you are not responsible for him giving in to sin, you are responsible for not meeting his needs if you withhold any good thing from him purposefully (Proverbs 3:27). You might have had a difficult day, but it is no excuse to punish your husband in this area. Talk and pray about it, take 15 to 20 minutes to refresh yourself and offer yourself up to him physically. Your monthly cycle is not an excuse to pull away from your husband either. You can use these times for growing closer together, holding each other in a non-sexual way, having important conversations, and dealing with lingering issues.

- **It's not About Physical Fitness**
  1 Samuel 16:7 states: *"Man looks at the outward appearance, but the Lord looks at the heart."* What has helped me be confident sexually is to keep eating healthy and remaining active. If, like me, you

have had children, your body has already changed. Striving to keep looking like you are 25 years old forever will not only waste your time, it will leave you frustrated, and does not honor God with the time He has given you. The aging process will happen no matter what amount of effort we put into trying to reverse the effects of time on our bodies. Having a flat stomach and calves of steel is not the key to healthy sexuality. It's about offering up what you already have to your husband to fulfill his needs.

- **Mutually Agree on How to Live out your Sexual Intimacy**
  How you choose to bring excitement into your routine is up to both of you. A principle we have applied in our marriage is that if one of us feels uncomfortable or disagrees about a certain issue, we abstain from practising it out of love for the other person.

Being honest is important as you surely do not want to start doing something out of pressure, but out of conviction that it is where the Lord is leading you and your husband. God convinces us, Satan pressures us.

If we read the *Song of Solomon*, we find that the lovers both marvel at each other's beauty and find fulfillment in simply being able to express their love through physical intimacy. I believe that is the essence of sexuality. Just as it is fun to eat cake on a birthday and it adds to the pleasure of the celebration. When it comes to sexuality, it is fun to have special nights once in a while, perhaps enjoy some romance. But trying to live out those moments constantly will leave you depleted of the original intent of creating a special bond between a husband and his wife. You could end up merely focusing on the preparation and miss what God wants to do between the two of you.

Some of the things mentioned in this chapter are possibly hard to take in. But if you are fully committed to God and to your marriage, everything is possible with God.

"What is impossible for man is possible for God"

Luke 18:27 (NLT)

After our wedding, being attentive to my husband's physical and emotional needs even with his ongoing immorality was a full-time commitment. I still devoted myself to honor him in this area no matter what. I trusted God with the outcome. I understood I couldn't pick and choose what parts of the Bible to obey. Out of love for my Savior, I gave all of myself, even when it was hard, even seeming impossible. I made sure my conscience was clear before my Maker in regard to our intimacy. I did not hide my pain or my hurts from Phil, but expressed them and made him know how much I longed to be one with him and him only. I shared how I desired to grow spiritually with him and wholeheartedly serve the Lord. I certainly don't do it perfectly, but the more I grow spiritually, the more I aim to please God in all the areas of my life, as best I can, leaning on Jesus, knowing that through the power of the Holy Spirit, all things are possible.

"For I can do everything through Christ
who strengthens me"

Philippians 4:13 (NLT)

As you seek to be faithful in your spiritual journey with the Lord, live in the present and for the future, leave the past behind you, holding only to the lessons it taught you. Give yourself wholly to God and watch what He can do in and through you!

CHAPTER FIFTEEN

SUFFERING AND BROKENNESS

"To believe in Him is not such a great thing.
To become like Him is truly great."

Richard Wurmbrand, *In God's Underground*

The plight of suffering has puzzled the world over and over again with the question of why God allows such a thing? Why would a good and loving God allow us to go through difficult, hard, and sometimes seemingly impossible situations? One of my favorite things is reading Christian biographies and testimonies. I truly enjoy reading about how God can change a person to such an extent you can hardly recognize them. They become truly alive, bold and change the world around them for Christ in such powerful ways, that no one is left indifferent to their message and way of life. It is such a marvelous encouragement to my own spiritual walk. Through the hard seasons of my marriage, it helped keep my focus in perspective, and even today I keep reading them. It has positively affected my walk in many ways.

One of the ways I came to understand suffering was through my own life. Once I looked back on my childhood, after coming to Christ, I could see my heavenly Father's hand over all my life circumstances. Had I experienced an easier, more comfortable, fun-filled and carefree life, I likely would have never met God in such a deep way. I am thankful today to have gone through all these difficult seasons and trials. I truly am.

The first time I picked up Reverend Richard Wurmbrand's book *Tortured for Christ*, it was a life-changing experience for me. It helped me see my marital struggles in a very different perspective. If this man, who endured persecution so intensely that he was unable to describe it all, could love his persecutors in such a deep way, who was I to complain about my own hardships? My issues seemed incredibly insignificant, and I began to understand the blessing of brokenness. Jesus' words began to take a whole new significance as I read them with this new perspective in mind. When hanging on the cross, with many spitting on Him, reviling Him and insulting Him, He prayed that His Father (God) would forgive them (Luke 23:34). He had such compassion on their state of utter brokenness that even through His own suffering, which was initiated by those very people, His heart broke for them. He knew the eternal ramifications of their actions and took no pleasure in knowing they would end up perishing because of their unbelief and coldness of heart.

Having children of my own also helped me see suffering in a different light. When you are trying to raise a child to the glory of God, it not only takes much energy and effort, but a heavenly perspective to be able to complete this task faithfully. If we simply go along in life letting them do whatever they wish, trying our best not to upset them too much, and be seen as nice and friendly parents, we will ruin their lives.

Phil and I understood from our own backgrounds that we needed to seriously consider how we wanted to raise our own children. What are our objectives for them? How do we want them to look when they leave home? What character qualities did we want to see them display? How were we going to give them a strong foundation to enable them to take a solid stand for Christ?

If God would allow us to wander through life aimlessly, without any unpleasant consequences, He would not be a loving God. Just as a loving parent disciplines its child, so does a loving God discipline us. He allows hardships and trials to refine and mold us. He sees the end picture and knows what it takes for us to get there.

> *"No discipline is enjoyable while it is happening—it's painful! But afterward there will be a peaceful harvest of right living for those who are trained in this way."*
>
> *Hebrews 12:11 (NLT)*

One way to short-circuit all the frustration of hardships in our lives is to begin seeing every single situation we find ourselves in as having been allowed by God for His greater purposes. When you accept this in your heart, not just your mind, life begins to take on a whole new, better meaning. In essence, that is the very meaning of faith.

Another thought about suffering that kept coming back to my mind was how I could possibly love my enemies if I couldn't even love my husband when he hurt me. And if God would allow me to suffer persecution, imprisonment or even torture, how could I love those people if I did not love my own husband as Christ loved him?

> *"Not all of us are called to die a martyr's death, but all*
> *of us are called to have the same spirit of self-sacrifice*
> *and love to the very end as these martyrs had."*
>
> Richard Wurmbrand, *The Midnight Bride*

We owe our lives to the Son of God. That's the reason, as we discussed in chapter 6, for the importance of laying down our lives. If you haven't laid down your life, it will be impossible to be joyful in the midst of trials, let alone love your husband through a hard season. You might end up wallowing in self-pity and resenting the very trial God is meaning to use to refine you and bring you to the next step of your walk with Him.

God's prompting has led me to share certain parts of my childhood with you. I believe that some of you need to heal from similar experiences and let go of the past in order to find healing through Jesus. When hurt, we tend to build walls around ourselves to prevent further hurt from affecting us. But this strategy is not effective, because it also prevents God from coming in and healing us. In this stage of false security, we position ourselves as very easy targets for Satan to lure us down a road full of self pity, victimhood, depression and the likes. As we learn to trust Him to heal us, these invisible walls come down and His Spirit moves in to begin the healing process. We are never more vulnerable than when we refuse access to the One who made us and possesses the only efficient power to rebuild our lives from the damage others, the enemy, and even ourselves have caused us.

Not only was our family distant, but living in a home where your parents are on bad terms is difficult. When drunk, my father would often scream at my mother and us, calling us names and swearing. He would tell us how he did not care about us and couldn't care less how we felt.

Sometimes objects flew into a crash and holes were punched in walls. Once, my father threatened to throw me down the stairs if I didn't give him the key to the car, which I refused to do as he was drunk. Careless words are very destructive. I would perform rather well in school, but every time I came home, I would get the same answer from my father: "You can do better next time!" This caused me for years to doubt I was doing enough. I became a people pleaser. It carried on in my early years as a Christian. I thought I had to do all sorts of things to earn God's favor. But that couldn't have been further from the truth, since God loves us as we are. He asks of us to turn wholeheartedly towards Him, to cry out to Him, and to trust and obey His leading. Our salvation depends purely on His grace.

Outside of work, my parents would entertain friends, attend social events through the embassies where we were posted, and watch television. On weekends where these things did not take place, they would sometimes take us to resorts. But even then, their interaction with us was minimal.

The tension in my parent's marriage escalated as I became older. In hindsight, I can clearly see Satan's heavy bondage on my parents. They did not know there was a way out of this unhealthy pattern.

Once we moved back to Canada in 1993, things became worse. My father was promoted to a new position, which led him to travel to embassies alone and be gone for weeks at a time. As a teenager, I could already see he was not exclusive to my mother. My father owned pornographic magazines and would make his thoughts known when he saw a beautiful woman. I was introduced to movies with romantic and sexual scenes at a young age. And with my father having a passion for horror movies, it left me very insecure and frightened. These things led to me suffering from insomnia very early in life. I can look back and see these were modes of escapism. Because the more the years went by, the more the tension became evident and heavy in our home. I could clearly see that modes of "escapism" were not effective, but instead aggravated the problems.

At the age of fifteen, we moved again and the next three years were very hard. My father's travelling became more frequent and it was obvious by then he was committing adultery. My mother also became increasingly angry at us. Memories of her hitting me on the head and forcefuly grabbing my arms still brings tears to my eyes. My mother was such a strong figure in my younger years, it was hard seeing her "cope" with her life circumstances this way. I understand today how her situation left her desperate for relief. Oh, how God can change a soul! I am so glad He did and cleansed my heart of these very damaging emotions and attitudes towards my mother.

Today my heart understands how miserable she was. She became so depressed when being home with us because of the ongoing turmoil surrounding her private life, that I was left to do most of the house chores, cut the grass, shovel the snow and even repair things around the house. As she was trying her best to make ends meet financially, I began helping my younger brother with his homework and attending parent-teacher meetings. I have since learned that when you encounter Jesus, you need not carry all these burdens as He wants to carry them with you, and step by step will set you free from them, if you allow Him.

Fast-forward a couple years into my marital issues. I began to understand why God had not intervened sooner during my childhood and rescued me out of my hardships. I realized I had not learned yet to turn to Him and was still wanting to do things my own way. Only when I acknowledged my desperate need for a Saviour did my life begin changing.

This summer (2021), Phil and I will be celebrating 20 years as a couple. Through all these years, only two times have I had a break for a day and a half on my own. Every single time we planned a time of refreshment for myself or as a couple, something serious happened. Twice we left for a weekend, but because of his sexual immorality, the time was mostly centered on physical intimacy. It left me depleted emotionally, but I chose to press on as I knew deep in my heart how Jesus was more than enough for me. I think most of those circumstances were orchestrated by the enemy in order to discourage me. But it didn't work. I pressed on, knowing that if God had allowed it, then He was going to carry me through it. I focused my thoughts on my eternity with Jesus instead of my present circumstances, knowing this side of life is but temporary.

And during those two times I actually had a break for myself, once I developed a nasty cold and ended up not sleeping at all, which led me to returning home more tired than before I left. The other time, two friends and I went to a cottage. When we got there, the kitchen was a mess, dirty and full of mildew. There was no running water, which required us to fill buckets of snow, and melt them in order to flush the toilet! When we finally went to bed, I noticed the roof was leaking and all through the night I could not sleep because of the constant dripping sound. So why am I telling you all this? Certainly not so you can pity me, but to tell you all things work for His good! God has used every single one of these circumstances to draw me to Himself, and give me a thankful heart.

"The school of life offers some difficult courses, but it is in the difficult class that one learns the most – especially when your teacher is the Lord Jesus Himself."

Corrie Ten Boom, *Tramp for the Lord*

When Phil was addicted to pornography, I couldn't make myself go out and leave the home very often. I am thankful God used me to protect my children. It was far more important eternally than an evening out, which was temporary. My relief and rest come from being and walking in His presence. Nothing in this world has *ever* given me the joy of intimate fellowship with my heavenly Father. Nothing. Things and occasions have filled my heart, but it is always temporary. What fills it permanently, no matter what He allows my way, is knowing I have a clear conscience before Him and that He loves me beyond what words can express. It greatly motivates me that every passing day I am closer to meeting my Savior face to face. Like Bart Millard says in his now famous song: *"I Can Only Imagine what it will be like!"*

I have learned the best lessons of my life in the middle of my hardships. There are times, I felt God so close, it was incredibly comforting. You and I need to remember that our lives are but a vapor. We **will** have trouble in this world. It might not seem like a vapor when you are going through it, but once we get to heaven and our lives never end, our perspective will be different. This life is momentary. It's a training ground for eternity. Paul compares our lives to a race and one day that race will be over. Who will be left standing at the finish line?

"They (Paul and Barnabas) encouraged them to continue in the faith, reminding them that we must suffer many hardships to enter the Kingdom of God."

Acts 14:22b (NLT, parenthesis mine)

Consider with me some of the quotes below, by men and women who learned firsthand what it means to suffer for Christ. God has used quotes and testimonies like these to shape my thinking about suffering. I love meditating on thoughts like those and letting God continue to change my heart.

- *"The deep meaning of the cross of Christ is that there is no suffering on earth that is not borne by God"*
  - Dietrich Bonhoeffer

- *"Even the best of Christians are troubled by the question, "Why does an Almighty God send, or at least allow, suffering?" When you are nagged by thoughts like this, say to yourself, "I am still in elementary school. When I graduate from the university of Christian life, I will understand His ways better and doubts will cease."*
  - Richard Wurmbrand

- *"If the church is most vibrant under trial and tribulation, why do we seek a life free of dangers?"* - Charles E. Moore and Timothy Keiderling, *Stories of Martyrdom and Costly Discipleship*

- *"He said there were two kinds of Christians: those who sincerely believe in God and those who, just as sincerely, believe that they believe. You can tell them apart by their actions in decisive moments."* - Richard Wurmbrand, *The Midnight Bride*

- *"One of the main ways we move from abstract knowledge about God to a personal encounter with him as a living reality is through the furnace of affliction."*
  - Timothy Keller, *Walking with God through Pain and Suffering*

- *"No healthy Christian ever chooses suffering, He chooses God's Will as Jesus did, whether it means suffering or not."*
  - Oswald Chambers

- *"If you look at the world, you'll be distressed. If you look within, you'll be depressed. If you look at God you'll be at rest."*
  - Corrie Ten Boom

- *"If your faith rests in your idea of how God is supposed to answer your prayers, your idea of heaven here on earth or pie in the sky or whatever, then that kind of faith is very shaky and is bound to be demolished when the storms of life hit it. But if your faith rests on the character of Him who is the eternal I AM, then that kind of faith is rugged and will endure."*
- Elisabeth Elliot, *Suffering Is Never for Nothing*

I am ending this chapter with a beautiful poem by Amy Carmichael.

We follow a scarred Captain,
Should we not have scars?
Under His faultless orders
We follow to the wars.
Lest we forget, Lord, when we meet,
Show us Thy hands and feet.

CHAPTER SIXTEEN

LIVING BY THE SPIRIT

"When a man is filled with the Holy Spirit,
he has vital power
That makes people know he has seen God.
He ought to be in such a place spiritually
that when he goes into a neighbor's house,
or out among people,
They will feel that God has come into their midst."

Smith Wigglesworth

What Christian wouldn't want the type of effect in their lives for Christ that Mr. Wigglesworth talks about? Look at the church in the book of Acts, it was on fire for God! It saddens me today when I know this is what God still wants for His church, and His people, yet few of us are ready, or available, or even desire that type of life. It is far from being an easy lifestyle. It is demanding, painful at times and some requests from the Father can leave you frazzled. But God makes no mistakes. What He asks of you He will help you carry through. What He asks He has approved and knows the eternal reward and growth in store for us if we obey Him.

Marital issues and the increasing divorce rate did not occur overnight. We have let our guard down as the Body of Christ and much of the church in North America now suffers from apathy. A lot of people have accepted the worldview around them almost as normal, and have let it corrupt their thinking. I am still astonished at the increasing political correctness permeating our churches today, lest we offend someone. And all the while keeping our mouths closed to the very truth that set us free in the first place. God did not call us to keep being part of the world, simply to keep living in it after salvation. We are to be light in the darkness, bringing salt where there is no flavour, where people have no taste for God, or have lost their appetite for it.

If we cannot bring ourselves to be light and salt in our own homes, as wives, we will never be effective outside of it. Our impact will be very minimal and certainly not the life-changing impact God desires to have through us when we walk in the fullness of His Spirit. The Pentecost experience, the coming of the Holy Spirit, was not an exclusive experience for the apostles only. It is still available to us today. God is the same yesterday, today and forever (Hebrews 13:8). His purpose for the church hasn't changed.

When going through hard seasons in marriage, where do you turn first? What is your initial reaction? Where do you go for help? While church programs, counselling, Bible studies, sermons and small groups are good things God can most certainly use to shape and mold us, they are not meant to replace our relationship with God and our dependence on His Holy Spirit. He should be where we first turn in the good and bad seasons, He should have first place in our search for help and guidance and our initial reaction should be to drop to our knees in prayer. Only when I seriously began to open up the Word did I develop a true hunger for God. Only when I was exposed to the Scriptures did I begin to change. Only when I began sincerely crying out for His help did it come. Only when I devoted quality time to spend in His presence did my life take a different turn and I began to experience joy in my trials. Only through my daily quiet time did I begin to see His ways were so much different than mine. Then He redirected me to exactly what I needed to grow in the areas of Bible studies, sermons, godly fellowship and help. But I first had to surrender to Him and His ways, and willingly choose not to lean on my own understanding. I waited for His timing in all these issues. I wanted to be transformed inside and out by Him and Him alone. No amount of godly material or study will ever have the impact of time spent in the presence of the Almighty. Nothing. And as the years have gone by, the thirst for His presence is only growing. Sometimes my heart cannot contain His amazing love for me. I marvel at how He is sufficient for all our needs, *nothing* is left out when we surrender to Him *exclusively*. I only have one Master and I must keep learning to follow where He leads.

*"The work of God can only be carried on by the power of God. The church is a spiritual organism fighting spiritual battles. Only spiritual power can make it function as God ordained. The key is not money, organization, cleverness, or education. Are you and I seeing the results Peter saw? Are we bringing thousands of men and women to Christ the way he did? If not, we need to get back to his power source. No matter the society, or culture, the city or town, God has never lacked the power to work through **available people** to glorify His name."*

Jim Cymbala, *Fresh Wind, Fresh Fire (emphasis mine)*

We are not all called to be used by God in the same way. Some of us will be called to testify and witness to many, some will be called to the mission field, some to lead a church congregation, and some of us will be called to be housewives. All are equally important. We are to be faithful where we are, where God has chosen for us to live. Remember our passage in chapter 2 about no coincidences? Acts 17:26-27 reminds us we are exactly where God intended us to be. And for all of us, no matter what the calling God has placed on our lives, our faithfulness in serving Him begins at home.

We might not lead thousands to Christ like the apostles did. But, the Great Commission (Matthew 28:19-20) is for **all** Christians. Ephesians 5:18 exhorts us to "be filled with the Spirit". The fact that it is written in the present tense indicates it's a state we should keep pursuing. While we cannot lose the indwelling, we can limit its power and affect by not walking closely with God. In Acts 2 the apostles received the Holy Spirit, then later in Acts 4 they were filled again with the Holy Spirit. Which implies that we can get fresh "fillings" every day. By becoming comfortable with the status quo, and by not allowing God to grow our faith, we then limit the power of the Spirit and keep ourselves from being refreshed and filled anew with divine power. The closer the Day of Jesus Christ approaches, the more we need to keep being filled in order to stand firm and not lose our footing. Lest we become complacent with simply knowing who Jesus is, having our sins forgiven, and having secured our place in heaven. That's a one-way relationship where we are in for benefits only, not growth or genuine change. The mental picture I carry of this concept is rooted in Jesus' words in Matthew 6:21: *"Wherever your treasure is, there the desires of your heart* *will also be."* I add to this mental picture the words of Paul in Galatians 5:16: " *So I say, let the Holy Spirit guide your lives. Then you won't be doing what your sinful nature craves."* I visualize a beautiful treasure chest where I put my most prized possession: my relationship with my Father in heaven. And every day I strive to keep filling this beautiful treasure chest with His love for me, His teachings, His comfort, His leading, His discipline. I often ask the Holy Spirit to fill me afresh so I can be a good representative of His grace to others. I ask Him to teach and show me how I can be a good wife and mother for that day and to the other people God chooses to put on my path for that day. And I hope to keep filling that chest with "fresh fillings" every day so it will help to carry me to the Day of Jesus Christ.

Our way of life should inspire people to seek Jesus. Our presence should reflect His love and entice people to ask how they can have what we have. You cannot give what you do not possess. Most unbelievers I have met are not looking for a sermon or a 12 point list on how to live the Christian life. They are hungry for relief, for healing, for love, for a listening ear, for a hug, and for compassion and mercy. They need to know Jesus is real. And you and I cannot convey that without the Holy Spirit. Only His presence in and through us can draw people to God. We need to be patient and understand that our role is to be available for God to speak and act through us. We are **not** to convince or pressure people to believe. That's the Holy Spirit's job. Otherwise we become a wall between God and people and greatly hinder His work, even push people away from Him. We will have to answer for that one day, if we don't repent and follow Him and His ways.

We might also see the work of God only being done inside a church building, perhaps only by pastors, ministry workers or missionaries. But actually it is meant to be everywhere we are, not contained in a building. As wives, our first ministry is to our home and family. And it can be the hardest place for us to live out the gospel. Living day in and day out with people who see every facet of our personality leaves no room for hypocrisy. We can think our husband and children cannot see through us. Just as we can see through them, so they can see through us. They can clearly tell if we are serious in our walk with Christ or not. How are we being an example to our husbands? How are we doing in our role as their helper?

And if we have children, how are we labouring to love and disciple them to follow Jesus?

We need to develop the same attitude Isaiah had when he encountered God, through a vision, at the Temple in Jerusalem: *"Here am I, send me!"* What if you and I had the same response? Here am I, Lord, send me, use me for your glory! May He remove the blinders off our eyes and let us become all that He intends us to be! May He mold us into the helpers our husbands need. May He show us how to handle family life His way, and teach us to follow the Spirit's leading. May He help us discern His voice, teach us how to pray without ceasing, and keep our eyes focused on Jesus, the author and perfecter of our faith. May He give us boldness to stand for Christ, even if it means standing alone. Give us courage to complete the work He chose to set before us, and give us the strength to not only finish this race, but finish it well. May we go where He sends us, depending on Him alone.

When our youngest, Sebastien, was in ICU after birth and then underwent open heart surgery, I had to wake up very early to pump breast milk in order to bring them a fresh supply every day. His situation was fragile at birth and no one knew where his breathing issues could lead or what would be the result. But every morning, before eating breakfast and heading out for the hospital, I spent an hour or more in the presence of God. I prayed, read His Word, and asked for His strength to be able to face what He had chosen for me to face on that day. I am glad I took the time to seek Him. I don't think I would have lasted very long in my own strength. I was sleeping about two to three non-consecutive hours a night. There is no way I made it through the first 15 months of Sebastien's life in my own strength.

He enabled me to witness to some people around me in the hospital. I even had the privilege of making a new friend and praying for her newborn daughter who suffered from severe heart arrhythmia. God answered my prayers by enabling the doctors to establish the proper medication dosage in the hours after my prayers. I do not possess any special ability, I simply prayed through the power of the Holy Spirit as I felt God's call on this precious little girl's life. I was recently informed by my friend, her mother, that she is off her medication and healed!

Marriage is the second most important relationship we will ever have, but God has plans for us and as Christians we cannot escape the Great

Commission call on our lives. We need to rely on our Heavenly Father to find balance in this world. We need to listen to His promptings and when He beckons a call on our lives for His Kingdom, we need to answer the call obediently and faithfully. Any area of your spiritual walk left to decay will hinder your witness for Christ, whether in your home or outside of it. Only through a life completely surrendered to Him can His Spirit bring forth His many blessings and His power.

God taught me something over the years that has incredibly blessed me. We very briefly touched on this point in chapter 11. I call it the "Guard Your Heart Above All Else Principle." The instant I feel a wrong attitude or thought welling up in me, I deal with it immediately. I do not let its roots develop and invade my heart and mind. It doesn't mean I am perfect and sinless. Far from that. Sometimes I am busy and my attention is not solely focused on what my husband or children are trying to convey, so I answer them without much thought or biblical wisdom. Most of the time it takes no more than 10 minutes before the Holy Spirit has convinced me to correct what just happened. On more difficult occasions, it may take a full day before my heart is softened. If you leave Him room, He *will* transform you. Some temptations will need an actual complete stop in our activities to retreat for prayer alone with the Father. Take that time as it is more precious than anything we could receive in this world. No matter where you are, even if you only have a bathroom or a closet, as I have used at times, it is better than nothing. Peace of mind cannot be bought, it demands much of our devotion in seeking it diligently. We cannot take shortcuts here as this type of attitude only demonstrates we are not genuine in our walk with Christ. It only reveals our own foolishness in thinking we can possess all the benefits and blessings of God without requiring any effort on our part. Jesus reminds us in John 10:27-28 that His sheep hear His voice and follow Him and He gives them eternal life. There are only two options in this world, you either follow Christ or you don't.

We desperately need revival, as individuals and as a church. Read again Jesus' prayer in John 17. The enemy is winning more and more territory every day. Marriage as God intended it is falling apart, divorce rates in the church are alarming, the family is being attacked like never before, and our human rights are being taken away from us bit by bit by governments. We do not need more church programs, or new laws, or to sign all the petitions thrown at us, or to march to claim our freedom of religion or speech. We need power from heaven! We need help from the One who commands Heaven's Armies. We need the same response Peter and John had when released from prison after preaching about Jesus in the temple area:

> *"**As soon** as they were freed, Peter and John **returned to the other** **believers** and told them what the leading priests and elders had said. When they heard the report, **all the believers lifted their voices together in prayer to God** [...] And now, O Lord, hear their threats, and **give us, your servants, great boldness in preaching your word**. Stretch out your hand with healing power; may miraculous signs and wonders be done through the name of your holy servant Jesus. After this prayer, the meeting place shook, and they were all filled with the Holy Spirit. Then they preached the word of God with boldness."*

> *(Acts 4:23-24a, 29-31, NLT, emphasis mine)*

They never asked for protection, comfort, or for their own agenda or ideas to be blessed. They did not ask for their rights or freedoms to be protected. They asked for power to carry the Great Commission with boldness. This is where you and I need to go. What is the state of our prayer lives as individuals and as a church? How patient are we to wait upon *His* answers? How much do we rely on His Holy Spirit to lead us? How faithful are we to obey? Jesus mentions several times in John 14 to 17 that if we love Him, we will obey Him. We are living in the last of the last days. We need to be faithful in our marriages, even if it means God calls us to suffer in them. We need to seriously heed Jesus's warning:

> *"Not everyone who calls out to me, 'Lord, Lord,' will enter the Kingdom of Heaven, but only those who actually do the will of my Father in heaven will enter. On judgement day many will say to me, 'Lord!, Lord! We prophesied in your name and cast out demons in your name and performed many miracles in your name.' But I will reply, 'I never knew you. Get away from me, you who break God's laws.'"(Matthew 7:21-23, NLT)*

That verse has been one of my life verses. It has driven me to seek my Father with all of my heart, soul, mind, and strength. I had to repent of wasting away His time, of neglecting to seek His will, and for being complacent about the lost, His people. And I had to begin in my own home, toward my husband and children. It led me down many hard seasons, but it drew me to the Throne of Grace time and time again. Troubles will come and go in this world and we need to accept that reality if we seek to follow Jesus. If you are not ready for that, you are not ready to follow Jesus. We also need to be ready for many detours, as the Holy Spirit is not restrained by our agendas. We need to be flexible and not tied to our own ideas of what we think we can do for God. We need to not plan and then ask God to bless it and beg for His help. If He is Lord of our lives, He gets to choose, not us. We need to ask God what His plans are and *then* ask Him to fill us afresh with the Spirit's power to carry out His plans. And above all, not to lean on our own understanding because His ways are *not* our ways. We are created in His image, but His ways are higher than ours, and His thoughts are higher than ours (Isaiah 55:8-9). Who can be His counselor? None of us! (Isaiah 40:13) For God is not led by sinners, but desires to lead sinners and turn them into saints for His glory. And in turn use them to revolutionize the world around them for His Kingdom.

Earlier this year (2021), God asked a very specific request of Phil and me. He woke me up 30 minutes before our usual alarm so I could clearly hear Him. He told us to write letters to the prostitutes Phil had committed adultery with and forgive every one of those ladies. The request led to many Spirit-led conversations between Phil and me and further healing for both of us. The Spirit's presence was very palpable. So we proceeded as God had instructed. Phil asked for forgiveness for using them as a source of temporary satisfaction. We then presented the Gospel to them and I personally ended the letter with a word of love. As I wrote those letters, I felt genuine love overflow my own heart for each of these ladies. Jesus stretched His arms on the cross for them as much as for you and me. Today I still pray for those ladies and I harbor no grudge against them. God wants to heal every fibre, corner, nook and crevasse in us. Are we letting Him do so?

"I desire that all of you be so filled with the Spirit, so hungry, so thirsty, that nothing will satisfy you but seeing Jesus. We are to get more thirsty every day, more dry every day, until the floods come and the Master passes by, ministering

to us and through us the same life, the same inspiration, so that "as He is, so are we in this world" (John 14:7). When Jesus became the sacrifice for man, He was in great distress, but it was accomplished. It meant strong crying and tears (see Hebrews 5:7); it meant the cross manward but the glory heavenward. Glory descending on a cross! Truly, "great is the mystery of godliness" (1 Timothy 3:16), He cried, "It is finished!" (John 19:30). Let the cry never be stopped until the heart of Jesus is satisfied, until His plan for humanity is reached in the sons of God being manifested (Romans 8:19) and in the earth being "filled with knowledge of the glory of the Lord, as the waters cover the sea" (Habbakuk 2:14). Amen. Amen. Amen." - Smith Wigglesworth, *"Smith Wigglesworth on the Holy Spirit."*

What would the church look like if you and I had this type of attitude? What would it look like to set foot in a church that is consumed with the heart of God to such an extent His presence is palpable? Where the people of God are so saturated with the love of Jesus, revival explodes everywhere they set foot. Where fingers are done pointing, where gossip has gone extinct, where looking down on others is a thing of the past, where hypocrisy has been buried, where complacency has died. Where holding grudges against one another and ignoring some people out of anger is not even a thought. Where forgiveness is extended no matter what the situation is as we understand how much we have been forgiven. Where no "exclusive" groups are formed, but where believers are of one heart and mind. Where mindless debates cease. Where Jesus reigns supreme and believers are hot, not lukewarm (because the lukewarm are not making it to heaven, see Revelation 3:16). Where believers understand we are all on the same road to heaven. Where believers actually become the church and not just attend one. Where the Holy Spirit is the first teacher and source of reliance. Where prayer is the primary mode of heavenly communication and where we all get our bread from above on how to advance His Kingdom His way here on earth. A place where God meets His people in a powerful, miraculous way.

We can rest assured that one day it will be this way - in heaven. Until then, each of us needs to make an individual, personal and conscious choice to live in a way that glorifies God in every aspect of our lives.

Change is possible and it starts with us in our own homes. Time is running out. What will you choose?

CHAPTER SEVENTEEN

GRACE AND HEALING

"'I have seen their ways, but I will heal them;
I will guide them and restore comfort to Israel's mourners,
creating praise on their lips.
Peace, peace, to those far and near,' says the Lord,
'And I will heal them.'"

Isaiah 57:18-19 (NLT)

Having finished chapter 16, you might rightfully ask, how do we experience a home or a church so consumed with the heart of God that His presence is palpable? As I was praying and asking God if I should add a conclusion or not, He answered by asking me to write another chapter. He asked me to share yet another lesson He has taught me and still carries me to this day. A lesson that took much time to invade all the corners of my heart. A lesson that I still need to let permeate every fiber of my body every day of my remaining life on earth. A lesson I have noticed many believers do not carry or do not know how to apply in their lives. A lesson we desperately need to understand in order to live the abundant life Jesus promises us (John 10:10b).

If you have been in church for any amount of time, you have certainly heard the word grace pronounced more than once. We use expressions frequently and often without fully transferring the actual rich and profound truth to our own hearts. "By the Lord's grace, we made it!" "By His grace we are saved!" "His grace is sufficient!" And many more similar expressions that include grace. One of the reasons so many believers in the church are struggling to extend grace, live in love with one another, or have genuine victory over sin is a failure to appropriate for themselves the very real and freeing gift of grace the Father lavished on us. Why couldn't

I offer grace to my husband in my early years as a Christian? Why couldn't I live the Christian life victoriously? Why did it take me over 6 years to make a complete commitment to Christ? Why was I experiencing so much insecurity in my walk with Christ? A major part of that was that I had not understood grace. I was also denying God access to the innermost parts of myself, which needed much healing and reprogramming.

Let me begin to unpack with you what the Holy Spirit has taught me on this subject and is still teaching me. Have you ever heard the expression, "Time heals all wounds?" Well, it is not true. Many wounds need a deeper, divine healing: rejection, humiliation, abandonment, parental neglect, trauma from the horrors of war or sexual abuse and more. In order to receive and experience healing in any of these areas, we must first understand what grace is. I noticed that a lot of Christian women, including myself, tend to put so much pressure on ourselves to look and act the part of a woman who has it all together. Often it is at our own expense. We are unable or unwilling to share what is really troubling us. That creates a "hole" in our faith and in our walk with Jesus Christ and we cannot experience His grace as He intended us to. These hurts, sins and difficulties become "infirmities" in our walk with Christ.

For example, I have had numerous women share with me privately how they were experiencing feelings or seasons of depression and low self-esteem. Some after childbirth, some after years of struggling through a broken marriage, some after being abandoned or neglected as a child and others after the death of a loved one. And in almost every case, these lovely ladies would confide how they felt depressed and ashamed because they believed depression had no place in the Christian life. Some blamed it on themselves, saying if they had more faith, they surely would not feel this way. Others were hurt by other Christians who assured them if they had more faith they would get out of that pit. Some were wrongly taught growing up, perhaps by parents who sincerely wanted to help them, but didn't have a rich relationship with Jesus or none at all. Some memories can leave scars for years, even decades. Hurtful words, public humiliation, a family member treating you wrongly, name calling, comparing you to another sibling in an unfavorable way, parents putting too many responsibilities on you. We could go on and on with this list.

Whatever your situation is, know that this is *not* the way Jesus sees you. He sees all of you, all your memories, all your hurts, all your sins, all your failures, all your damaged emotions, all the pain others inflicted upon you and all your future, and He loves you just *as you are*! He is *not* expecting you to change before you come to Him or make a recommitment. He is *not* expecting you to work harder at increasing your faith. He is *not* asking you to serve more in order to please Him. He is *not* expecting perfection from you in all the areas of your life. He desires you to come to Him *as you are*. Through His Spirit, He will direct your healing, He will allow situations in your life to increase your faith, and He will show you what *His plan and purpose* is for *your life*. This is the essence of my message to you, conveyed through the chapters of this book.

I understand many messages we hear from others can seem to contradict these principles. Past baggage, damaged emotions and unhealed memories can also affect how we respond to certain messages. There can be such a great emphasis in some churches to serve, serve, serve, but little or no emphasis on inner healing in order to experience the fullness of what God has in store for us. No church or ministry will ever be truly effective if most of its people are walking with spiritual "infirmities". If many of our churches are filled with "infirmities", how can we effectively be Christ's ambassadors? How can people come to be healed when we are walking with crutches ourselves? We need that power from heaven we talked about in the previous chapter. I understand we will only experience complete freedom and rest once Jesus comes again, but we can experience an incredible amount of freedom on this side of life as well. I sincerely believe that too many of us walk with so much emotional and spiritual "infirmities" that it prevents us from being truly effective in our witness and service for Christ. Satan would love nothing more than for each of us to keep carrying these "infirmities," for he knows full well the damage they keep doing. Left untreated they can even affect your physical health in damaging ways. Caroline Leaf, a Christian medical specialist, wrote a book called *Who Switched Off My Brain?* She notes interestingly, that how a person thinks affects their health and general well-being. This year (2020-2021), as part of our homeschool, we went through a curriculum called *Health and Nutrition* where the author Dr. Laura Chase shares similar medical findings.

Even Dan Dehaan's quote at the beginning of chapter 11 tells us that what we allow to preoccupy our minds will affect us at every level. So how do we experience victory and be *"transformed by the renewing of our minds?"* (Romans

12:1-2) We covered this in detail in chapters 5 and 11, that only through a rich, intimate relationship with God is this possible. I need to reiterate that there are no shortcuts here. If you still struggle with the concept of grace, I highly recommend meditating on the first two chapters of Ephesians. Here are some verses to help you understand who you are in Christ:

*"**Even before He made the world, God loved us and chose us** in Christ to be holy and without fault in His eyes. God decided in advance to adopt us into His family by bringing us to Himself through Jesus Christ. This is what He wanted to do, and it gave Him great pleasure. So we praise God for the glorious grace He has poured on us who belong to His dear Son. He is so rich in kindness and grace that He purchased our freedom with the blood of His Son and forgave our sins. He has showered His kindness on us, along with all wisdom and understanding."*

Ephesians 1:4-8 (NLT, emphasis mine)

Though we are not called to understand all of God's ways, in order to grow in our faith, we must start believing what He says in His Word. If we try to rationalize every verse, we will feel defeated. We are called to believe what He says, not become dissectors of God's Word. Just like a young child instinctively believes its parent when he answers his questions, so are we to believe our Father in heaven. Satan brings in doubts and wants us to question everything. By doing this, we will not be able to let the Word of God dwell richly in us (Colossians 3:16), since we seek to "understand" it before accepting it. But it is contrary to His ways since when we accept it by faith, He then helps us grow into a deeper knowledge of Himself and His ways. Only then are we positioned to begin our healing journey and experience greater freedom in our walk with Christ. A good read that convicted me is John Bunyan's *Holy War*. If you enjoy more modern English, Ethel Barrett has rewritten it and titled it *War for Mansoul*.

Drawing from the above verses in Ephesians, here are some amazing truths about how God thinks of us and how we are incredibly precious in His eyes:

- Before He made the world, He *loved* YOU and *chose* YOU.
- He decided ***in advance*** to adopt YOU into His family.

- He wanted YOU in His family.
- Adopting YOU brought Him **great** *pleasure.*
- He is **rich** in kindness and grace towards YOU.
- He forgave **all** your sins. Completely! Really! Seriously!
- He showered His kindness on YOU.
- He showered all His wisdom on YOU.
- He showered all His understanding on YOU.

Notice how the verbs in these statements are in the past tense. All these things were accomplished through the sacrifice of Jesus at the Cross. It was finished then. This is grace. Jesus did not attach prerequisites before we could experience grace and freedom. He only asks us to believe.

> *"Jesus called a little child to Him and put the child among them. Then he said, 'I tell you the truth, unless you turn from your sins and become like little children, you will never get into the Kingdom of Heaven. So anyone who becomes as humble as this little child is the greatest in the Kingdom of Heaven'"*
>
> *Matthew 18:2-4 (NLT)*

We desperately need to become more *childlike* in our faith and simply believe what the Word of God says. Stop debating it, voicing our opinions about it, or adapting it to our own liking to fit our agendas. Let's be like little children and humbly come at the feet of our Savior and accept all He so graciously showers on us. We know we don't deserve it, but we need not live in condemnation the rest of our lives (Romans 8:1). Doing so might keep you out of the Kingdom as we are accepting the lie that Jesus is not enough, that His sacrifice wasn't enough to save us, and that our sins are too great to be completely forgiven. Then we become *childish* in our walk with Christ. A good read here would be David A. Seamands' *Putting Away Childish Things.*

> *"When I was a child, I spoke and thought and reasoned as a child. But when I grew up, I put away childish things."*
>
> *1 Corinthians 13:11 (NLT)*

Healing depends on your acceptance of your identity as a child of God. We are still called a *child* of God, but have grown from our *childish* knowledge of this temporary world to a greater, more adult and eternal knowledge of our Creator, our Father in Heaven. If God showers His wisdom and His understanding on us (Ephesians 1:4-8, quoted above), we cannot remain *childish*. God's ways are not *childish*, they are made to make us more like Christ.

Once you know who you are in Christ, nothing will be impossible for you (Luke 18:27, Philippians 4:13). Forgiveness, repentance, loving others in a manner worthy of Christ, walking in the fullness of His Spirit and divine healing are all at your fingertips! Your faith will grow substantially and you will begin to experience such healing you never thought possible. Long kept memories of past hurts will start to vanish from your ruminating negative thinking as you ask God to pull down all the strongholds in your life. You will position yourself to be led by the Spirit as He wishes to uncover and expose hurtful patterns which are preventing you from letting go of your spiritual and emotional "infirmities." You will be able to point others to Christ with more ease, and will be amazed at how the Spirit is able to use you.

God is looking for ordinary people, not people who think they have it all together (Mark 2:17, Luke 5:31). It is *not* more theological knowledge, more classes and diplomas that make you an instrument for the Lord. It's a life totally and humbly surrendered to Him. Then you can victoriously put on the full armor of God and stand your ground against the enemy, firmly planted in your identity. Praying with all kinds of prayers, while you are standing, ask God to reveal Himself to you, His plan for *your* life, to make you bold for Christ and to allow you to be a strong and immovable daughter of the King of kings!

All I have shared with you through the chapters of this book are possible only through a complete acceptance of who we are in Christ. You will understand that there are no coincidences in this world.

- You will be able to remove the plank from your own eye and receive God's grace.
- You will make yourself available for the help and the hope offered to you in Christ Jesus.
- You will find strength in His presence.

- You will be able and willing to lay down your life and truly experience the abundant life Jesus promises us in John 10:10.
- You will have victory over your sinful nature and Satan's schemes.
- You will become increasingly perseverant.
- You will understand what God expects of you as a Christian wife and how to live out His plan in your marriage and your life.
- You will be naturally drawn to spend more quality time alone in His presence.
- You will be able to extend Christ's love in your marriage and life.
- You will be able to extend complete forgiveness and repent from all your hidden secrets, which are holding you captive.
- You will be able to live out your marital sexuality free of the world's pressures and ideas and be able to experience incredible oneness with your husband.
- You will begin to see suffering and brokenness as gifts to draw you into a closer relationship with your heavenly Father and sharing in Christ's sufferings.
- You will experience what it means to walk in the fullness of the Holy Spirit.
- You will be in a position to be healed and become a helper to others, thus enabling you to bear much fruit.

I could not end this chapter without sharing some practical ways God, through His holy Spirit taught me about healing damaged emotions:

- **Open up and Face your Problems**
  This is the first step to healing. Admitting you are struggling in one or more areas. Then taking responsibility for seeking godly help and possibly counselling like mentioned in chapter 4. While Jesus did send the Holy Spirit as our Helper, we are not meant to live our Christian life solo. The word 'church' in our English language means *gathering* or *assembly*. The Holy Spirit often uses a human counsellor to point out the root of our spiritual and emotional problems. While the human counsellor is only meant to be temporary, he is often used by God to help relieve our burdens, correct us, and teach us how to renew our minds in Christ.

- **Take Responsibility to Fix what Needs to be Changed**

  If you are holding onto a grudge, anger or hatred, you need to be honest about it. Through prayer, with a pastor or your counsellor, ask the Holy Spirit to direct you to the root of the problem. Perhaps this comes from broken childhood memories or hurtful situations in your marriage and it has permeated your thinking to such an extent it prevents you from experiencing victory over sinful patterns because of your damaged emotions. We live in a fallen world and around sinners, we are inevitably going to get hurt. But what we choose to hold on to will lead to spiritual success or defeat.

  Damaged emotions take time to heal. Give yourself grace. There is no shame in struggling, in fact, it is actually freeing to let all those broken emotions out. It is a sign you are on your healing journey. I still have days where I struggle from the pain of our marital issues. I trust that even though I don't always "feel" healing taking place, that God is at work through His Spirit in me. Because once those "episodes" take place and have gone by, I always feel lighter and freer.

  We also need to make a very important choice not to ruminate too long on past damaged emotions or painful memories. When we feel dejected for periods of time, that's when we need to make a very conscious effort to remember and appropriate the promises God has given us. Think and pray about these issues, but don't let your life be ruled by those damaging past events.

- **Apply Romans 8:26-30 to your Prayer Life**

  Often we do not know what to pray for, since only the Spirit knows everything about us, even what is stored deep into our subconscious minds. He knows what is holding us back or what prevents us from being fruitful in our marriages and in life. He can help us pray God's will when we do not know what to pray for.

  "And the Holy Spirit helps us in our weakness. For example, we don't know what God wants us to pray for. But the Holy Spirit prays for

us with groanings that cannot be expressed in words. And the Father who knows all hearts knows what the Spirit is saying, for the Spirit pleads for us believers in harmony with God's own will. And we know that God causes everything to work together for the good of those who love God and are called according to His purpose for them. For God knew His people in advance, and He chose them to become like His Son, so that His Son would be the firstborn among many brothers and sisters. And having chosen them, He called them to come to Him. And having called them, He gave them right standing with Himself. And having given them right standing, He gave them His glory." (Romans 8:26-30, NLT)

The verses previously mentioned in chapter 2 from Acts 17:26 - 27 state: *"From one man he created all the nations throughout the whole earth. He decided beforehand when they should rise and fall, and he determined their boundaries. His purpose was for the nations to seek after God and perhaps feel their way toward him and find him—though he is not far from any one of us."*

All that happened in your life and mine was allowed so that we would seek God and come into a personal relationship with Him. This is what God means when He says that *all things work for the good of those who love God and are called according to His purpose.* And *He is not far from any of us* and *having chosen us, He called us to come to Him.* And having chosen us, *He gave us right standing with Himself.* And *having given us right standing with Him, He gave us His glory.*

"So all of us who have had that veil removed can see and reflect the glory of the Lord. And the Lord—who is the Spirit—makes us more and more like him as we are changed into his glorious image." (2 Corinthians 3:18, NLT)

- **Extend to Others the Grace Given to you by Christ**
  Once you fully understand who you are in Christ, and have taken time to start healing, it becomes much easier to extend the same

grace we have received to others and to our own husbands. It is incredibly freeing to do so, it lifts a very heavy burden off our shoulders when we willingly choose to let go of everything our husbands might have done or might still be doing to us. You can begin to see your husband more clearly in a very different light when you harbor no grudge or negative feelings towards him.

An important note would be to remember that these feelings have a way of creeping back into our lives, often when we least expect it, even after we begin our healing journey. We live in a fallen world, carry a sinful nature until our death, and face an unseen but powerful enemy. So these feelings will inevitably arise more than once. But as we bring them into submission and captive to the obedience of Christ, they will slowly diminish over time.

What greater privilege could we want or need than God's grace freely given to us through Christ? The Holy Spirit has all the keys to the storehouses of our Father in heaven. All the heavenly treasures we will ever need are administered by the Holy Spirit through Christ. We need to stop simply talking about Him and actually start following Him wherever He leads us. The Holy Spirit is with us when we are thirsty for His presence, His help, His guidance, His wisdom and His understanding. He associates with childlike, faithful, and humble believers.

My dear Sister in Christ, I know all these things that I have written to you in this book are possible because I have experienced them personally. As I have said throughout this book it is not easy, but it is so worth it! You are loved! I am really looking forward to meeting you either in this life or in heaven. In the meantime, remember:

"Therefore we do not lose heart. Though outwardly we are wasting away, yet inwardly we are being renewed day by day. For our light and momentary troubles are achieving for us an eternal glory that far outweighs them all. So we fix our eyes not on what is seen, but on what is unseen, since what is seen is temporary, but what is unseen is eternal."

2 Corinthians 4:16-18 (NLT)

CONCLUSION

"Those who look to Him for help will be radiant with joy."

Psalm 34:5a (NLT)

This is the end of our journey together. I hope and pray it represents a new beginning for you and your marriage. Even if your situation doesn't change, I pray your heart and mind have been renewed. Let us remember where we came from and how much Christ has done for us through the lyrics of this beautiful hymn titled *All I have is Christ:*

> "But as I ran my hell-bound race
> Indifferent to the cost
> You looked upon my helpless state
> And led me to the cross
> And I beheld God's love displayed
> You suffered in my place
> You bore the wrath reserved for me
> Now all I know is grace
> Hallelujah! All I have is Christ
> Hallelujah! Jesus is my life"

(*All I have is Christ,* by Jordan Kauflin)

Let us forever boast in Him and Him only! Jesus **is** *The Way, The Truth and The Life!*

"God is not interested in good starters, He is interested in good finishers!"

Angus Buchan

"Our responsibility is faithfulness in service, not in results.
God alone is responsible for the results."

Dr. Charles Stanley

WHAT DO I NEED TO DO TO BE SAVED ?

You may have realized you cannot continue living the way you are at the moment. If so, that's the first step and a very important one.

*"Yet God has made everything beautiful for its own time. **He has planted eternity in the human heart,** but even so, people cannot see the whole scope of God's work from beginning to end."*

Ecclesiastes 3:11 (NLT)

When God created human beings in His own image (Genesis 1:26), He also set eternity in their hearts (see above verse). This means that deep in our hearts, most people know a God exists, even though they do not live for or acknowledge Him. If that weren't so, we wouldn't have all the multitude of world religions present today. People are searching for truth, peace, and perhaps a guarantee of eternal life. The Good News is it and all available! Jesus, God's one and only Son died on the cross that you might be reconciled to your Heavenly Father, God.

Following a very logical pattern, we need to understand that not all roads lead to Heaven. Just like a company could never be run by multiple CEOs who would all have their way to make the company function, while at the same time carry the same level of authority. This type of company would surely end up in complete chaos in a very short time. Why? A company needs order to function properly. Employees need to know who's in charge and who to follow.

The same is true for us human beings. To obtain peace in our lives, we need to appropriate ourselves with the Truth. Again, there cannot be multiple versions of the Truth. Otherwise, it would mean that anything goes! Whatever you choose to be true would be true. I could start worshiping a peanut butter sandwich, a dandelion or a plastic container all the days of my life, bow to them and expect to get into Heaven just because I believe it. That might sound ludicrous and far stretched, but when we reject the notion of an absolute Truth, we are saying anything goes.

God loves you more than you will ever know or understand. He wants you to experience peace and an eternal, fulfilling life right now. He went to great lengths to demonstrate His love for YOU.

> *"For God so loved the world, that he gave his one and only Son, that whoever believes in him should not perish but have eternal life." John 3:16 (NIV)*

He doesn't just love YOU, He *so* loves YOU.

> *"I came that they may have life and have it abundantly."*
> *John 10:10 (NIV)*

> *"We have peace with God through our Lord Jesus Christ."*
> *Romans 5:1 (NIV)*

Why don't most people have this peace and the fulfilling and abundant life that God intends for us to have?

Step ONE: Admit you are a sinner

That might be hard to read or admit, but it's the truth. None of us is righteous enough to save our own lives. If we are honest, we know we fall short, and know our shortcomings all too well. God created us in His own image (Genesis 1:26) and not like robots who automatically and mechanically obey Him. He also gave us a will and the freedom to choose. And when we choose to live our own way, this results in separation from God.

The Bible says:

> *"For all have sinned and fall short of the glory of God."*
> *Romans 3:23 (NIV)*

> *"For the wages of sin is death." Romans 6:23 (NIV)*

Death. Yes, spiritual death, and complete separation from God in this life and for eternity. We might argue that we have good intentions, but that is not enough.

"There is a way that seems right to a man, but its end is the way to death."

Proverbs 14:12 (NIV)

"Your iniquities have made a separation between you and your God..." Isaiah 59:2 (NIV)

"Not a single person on earth is always good and never sins." Ecclesiastes 7:20 (NLT)

We need to admit it is impossible to save ourselves. Our "good works" and "good intentions" cannot clear our record of sins and buy us eternity. God is Holy and He alone sets the standards of righteousness. God is also just and cannot let our sins go unpunished. But God knows we cannot save ourselves. In His immense and perfect love, He sent His Son, Jesus, to die for us and take the punishment for our sins. Jesus willingly came to earth to save You and me. It is a gift and cannot be bought, but freely offered to anyone who believes.

Step TWO: Believe!

Jesus Christ died on the cross and rose from the dead. Though He is God's sinless Son, He became a human, took our place, and paid the penalty for our sin, therefore demolishing the barrier between God and us. He is alive today and in heaven.

"Jesus answered, "I am the way and the truth and the life. No one comes to the Father except through me." John 14:6 (NIV)

"For, there is one God and one Mediator who can reconcile God and humanity—the man Christ Jesus." 1 Timothy 2:5 (NLT)

"Christ suffered for our sins once for all time. He never sinned, but he died for sinners to bring you safely home to God. He suffered physical death, but he was raised to life in the Spirit." 1 Peter 3:18 (NLT)

"I passed on to you what was most important and what had also been passed on to me. Christ died for our sins, just as the Scriptures said. He was buried, and He was raised from the dead on the third day, just as the Scriptures said."

1 Corinthians 15:3-4 (NLT)

"Yet God, in his grace, freely makes us right in his sight. He did this through Christ Jesus when he freed us from the penalty for our sins. For God presented Jesus as the sacrifice for sin. People are made right with God when they believe that Jesus sacrificed his life, shedding his blood. This sacrifice shows that God was being fair when he held back and did not punish those who sinned in times past,"

Romans 3:24-25 (NLT)

"But God showed his great love for us by sending Christ to die for us while we were still sinners."

Romans 5:8 (NLT)

God has provided the only way for the forgiveness of sin and eternal life. But each person must make a choice.

Step THREE: Receive Christ as your Savior

You must trust Jesus Christ as your Savior and receive Him by personal choice. He is waiting for you to come to Him that He might cleanse you from all unrighteousness and give you the peace you desperately seek.

"Look! I stand at the door and knock. If you hear my voice and open the door, I will come in, and we will share a meal together as friends."

Revelation 3:20 (NLT)

"To all who did receive him, who believed in his name, he gave the right to become children of God."

John 1:12 (NIV)

"And anyone who believes in God's Son has eternal life. Anyone who doesn't obey the Son will never experience eternal life but remains under God's angry judgment." Romans 3:36 (NLT)

What is your decision?

If you have been convicted of your own sins and realize your need for a Savior, you might want to pray and confess with your mouth your great need for Jesus Christ. I have included the following prayer. You can use it word-for-word or as an example.

"Heavenly Father, I come to You asking for the forgiveness of my sins. I confess with my mouth and believe in my heart that Jesus died on the Cross to pay the penalty for my sins. I recognize my great need for Jesus Christ to come into my life in order to become my Lord and Savior. I renounce my former way of life and seek today to honor You in all my ways. Please show me how to please You. Please heal the brokenness in my life and teach me to love others Your way. I thank You for making a way that I can be reconciled to You. Amen."

Rejoice! You are now a Child of God! A Daughter of the King of Kings!

Now that you have begun your new life with Jesus as your Savior, you will want to find a church near you that teaches the truth from the Word of God and whose leadership follows the Lord Jesus Christ. If you don't have a Bible, find out from someone at church where you can purchase or borrow one and begin spending time each day reading the Word of God on your own and talking to God through prayer. These things will help you to grow in your new faith and knowledge of Jesus as you start your own journey following Him.

EQUIPPING THE NEXT GENERATION OF WOMEN

If you have daughters like me, whether biological or adopted, you will want to impart the importance of representing Christ well both in and out of the home. What greater inheritance could we pass on to the next generation of women? Our sons are as important, but since this book focused solely on how we can represent Christ well in our marriages as wives, I chose to focus on our daughters. There are many good Christian books on the market on how to train our sons to be godly.

But it doesn't stop at our daughters only. You might be a foster Mom or have the privilege of shepherding and ministering to young ladies. God has put certain people on our path for a specific reason. Some for a season, some for life. How are we representing Him to the younger generation of women around us?

Be assured I need to be reminded as much as you. Daily life can become chaotic and it is easy to lose our eternal focus. That's the reason we discussed the importance of having quality time with our Savior in chapter 11.

One thing that has helped me remain focused is to envision what I would like my daughters to look like when they leave our home. I am not going to offer you a plan or solution in order to do this well. Instead, let us come to God and ask Him what His plans are regarding the young women He has placed in our lives. Here are some of the questions I ask myself and bring to God in prayer:

- What do I model in my everyday life?
- Can they tell I am genuinely walking in faith?
- How do I talk to them? Lovingly or harshly?
- Can they see evidence of Jesus in me?

- Do I spend enough quality time with them?
- Do I spend time teaching them the ways of God?
- Do I pray for them? Earnestly or sparingly?
- Do I listen well when they come to me?
- Have I surrendered them to God or do I hold onto them?
- When they do wrong, am I quick to pray or scold them?
- Am I quick to forgive them?
- Do I keep watch over them diligently?

I am certain you could add your own questions to these. But I don't stop at asking myself these questions. I ask God how He thinks I am doing in these areas. His answers can be favorable, convict me of my failures, or show me things I had not seen in my daughters that need to be addressed. He alone perfectly knows all the young ladies in my life. How faithful am I to bring them to the Throne of Grace and petition the Father on their behalf? How often do I think of the inheritance I am passing on to them?

Let us be bright lights to the young ladies in our lives!

Here are some ministries that have helped me shepherd my three daughters in all areas of life:

- Tomorrow's Forefathers: www.tomorrowsforefathers.com
- Doorposts: www.doorposts.com
- Solve Family Problems: www.solvefamilyproblems.org
- Girl Talk Home: www.girltalkhome.com
- Purity Works: www.purityworks.org
- Truth 78: www.truth78.org
- Answers in Genesis: www.answersingenesis.org
- Ultimate Goal Publications: www.stayinthecastle.com

LIST OF RESOURCES

I have compiled a list of books and resources, arranged by subject, that could possibly be of help in your spiritual and marital walk with Christ. These books **in no way replace** the truth of the Word of God, but can be used as guides and for practicality. Many of the authors use personal experience which readers can relate to.

1. **Marriage**
   Sacred Marriage, by Gary Thomas
   The Marriage Covenant : The Biblical Secret for a Love that Lasts, Derek and Ruth Prince
   You and Me Forever, Francis and Lisa Chan
   Divine Design: God's Complementary Roles for Men and Women, John MacArthur
   Feminine Appeal: Seven Virtues of a Godly Wife and Mother, Carolyn Mahaney
   The Excellent Wife, Martha Peace
   Gender and Sexuality, DVD sermons series by Charles Price, Living Truth

2. **Womanhood**
   Beauty in the Heart, Pam Forster
   The Lost Art of True Beauty, Leslie Ludy
   Set-Apart Woman, Leslie Ludy
   Set-Apart Femininity, Leslie Ludy

3. **Spiritual Growth**
   The Gospel According to Jesus, John MacArthur
   Hear God's Voice, Derek Prince
   The Knowledge of the Holy, A.W. Tozer

The Pursuit of God, A.W. Tozer
God's Pursuit of Man, A.W. Tozer
Sodom Had No Bible, Leonard Ravenhill
The Beast or The Lamb : Discerning the Nature That Determines Your Destiny, Derek Prince
If, Amy Carmicheal
Boundaries, Henry Cloud and John Townsend
The Four Loves, C.S. Lewis
The Imitation of Christ, Thomas A. Kempis
The Pursuit of Holiness, Jerry Bridges
The God You Can Know, Dan DeHaan
Living as Salt and Light, Derek Prince
Reaching Your Full Potential for God, Charles F. Stanley
Spiritual Disciplines of the Christian Life, Donald Whitney
Life Principles, DVD sermons series by Charles F. Stanley
Living in the Will of God, DVD sermons series by Charles Price

4. **Struggles / Dealing with Sins**
Pulling Down Strongholds, Derek Prince
Pride Versus Humility, Derek Prince
Exchanging Mirrors: A Call to Embrace your God-Given Identity, Katherine Hager
Freedom from Addiction, Neil T. Anderson, Mike Quarles
How to let God Solve your Problems, Charles F. Stanley
Respectable Sins, Jerry Bridges
Emotions : Confront the Lies, Conquer with Truth, Charles F. Stanley
The Gift of Forgiveness, Charles F. Stanley
Surviving in an Angry World, Charles F. Stanley
So Long Insecurity, Beth Moore
Lies Women Believe, Nancy Leigh De Moss
Are You Angry? Free PDF Book, Larry Darby (*www.solvefamilyproblems.com*)

5. **Holy Spirit**

   The Silent Shepherd, John MacArthur
   One Holy Fire, Nicky Cruz
   Smith Wigglesworth on the Holy Spirit, Smith Wigglesworth
   Holy Spirit in You, Derek Prince
   A Rushing Mighty Wind, Angus Buchan
   The Gifts of the Spirit, Derek Prince
   What Happens When God Pours Out Fresh Power, Jim Cymbala
   Fresh Wind, Fresh Fire, Jim Cymbala

6. **Prayer**

   Secrets of a Prayer Warrior, Derek Prince
   Spiritual Disciplines of the Christian Life, Donald Whitney
   Prayer : The Ultimate Conversation, Charles F. Stanley
   In Everything By Prayer, A.W. Tozer
   Utter Dependency on God Through Prayer, Bud Burk, Truth 78
   Ministries

7. **Intimacy**

   Passion and Purity, Elizabeth Elliott
   Sex and the Supremacy of Christ, John Piper

8. **Spiritual Warfare**

   The Invisible War: What Every Believer needs to know about Satan,
   Demons, and Spiritual Warfare, Chip Ingram
   The Believer's Armor, John MacArthur
   The Spiritual Warfare Answer Book, David Jeremiah

9. **Healing**

   Healing for Damaged Emotions, David. A. Seamands
   Healing of Memories, David A. Seamands
   Healing Grace: Freedom from the Performance Trap, David A.
   Seamands
   Putting Away Childish Things: Reaching for Spiritual and Emotional
   Maturity in Christ, David A. Seamands
   Pulling Down Strongholds, Derek Prince

10. **Brokenness / Suffering**

   Suffering is Never for Nothing, Elizabeth Elliott
   Suffering and the Sovereignty of God, John Piper
   The Problem of Pain, C.S. Lewis
   Walking with God Through Pain and Suffering, Timothy Keller

11. **Christian Life Metaphors**

   The Pilgrim's Progress, John Bunyan
   War for Mansoul: A John Bunyan Classic as told by, Ethel Barrett
   The Celestial Railroad, Nathaniel Hawthorne

This is the end of journey together!

But... I would love to hear from you!

You can write to me at :

<u>immovablewife@gmail.com</u>

Always remember... you are loved beyond
your wildest imagination!

Printed in the United States
by Baker & Taylor Publisher Services